AF683319

# DERIVATIVES DIARY

# DERIVATIVES DIARY

*The Strategies of an Independent Fund Manager*

RICHARD FOLCKER

JOHN WILEY & SONS, LTD
Chichester · New York · Weinheim · Brisbane · Singapore · Toronto

Copyright © 2001 John Wiley & Sons Ltd,
Baffins Lane, Chichester,
West Sussex PO19 1UD, England

National 01243 779777
International (+44) 1243 779777
e-mail (for orders and customer service enquiries):
cs-books@wiley.co.uk
Visit our Home Page on http://www.wiley.co.uk

All Rights Reserved. No part of this publication may be reproduced, stored in a retrieval system, or transmitted, in any form or by any means, electronic, mechanical, photocopying, recording, scanning or otherwise, except under the terms of the Copyright, Designs and Patents Act 1988 or under the terms of a licence issued by the Copyright Licensing Agency, 90 Tottenham Court Road, London, W1P 9HE, UK, without the permission in writing of the publisher.

Richard Folcker has asserted his right under the Copyright, Designs and Patents Act 1988 to be identified as the author of this work.

*Other Wiley Editorial Offices*

John Wiley & Sons, Inc., 605 Third Avenue,
New York, NY 10158-0012, USA

Wiley-VCH Verlag GmbH, Pappelallee 3,
D-69469 Weinheim, Germany

John Wiley & Sons Australia, Ltd, 33 Park Road, Milton,
Queensland 4064, Australia

John Wiley & Sons (Asia) Pte Ltd, 2 Clementi Loop #02-01,
Jin Xing Distripark, Singapore 129809

John Wiley & Sons (Canada) Ltd, 22 Worcester Road,
Rexdale, Ontario M9W 1L1, Canada

***British Library Cataloguing in Publication Data***

A catalogue record for this book is available from the British Library

ISBN 0-471-49771-1

Typeset in 10.5/13.5pt Tiepolo by Footnote Graphics, Warminster, Wiltshire
Printed and bound in Great Britain by Antony Rowe Ltd, Chippenham, Wiltshire
This book is printed on acid-free paper responsibly manufactured from sustainable forestation, for which at least two trees are planted for each one used for paper production.

To the three musketeers
Johan, Erik and Gustav

*who are a constant source of*
*love and inspiration*

# CONTENTS

February 2002

Dear Reader

I am Thomas R Jones and in front of you is my diary, which I wrote before and during the start-up and first year of running my own fund management firm, Thomas R Jones Investments Ltd. Since starting my own business was such a big step for me, I decided to record what I was about do – the process, events and what my feelings, thoughts and challenges were as well as how I was doing as an independent fund manager. I don't want to disclose too much here, but I can say that I have had an amazing year – ups as well as downs – and you have the opportunity to read about them in this book.

However, I have the chance here to present myself to you and I'm not a man who often misses opportunities. I am 42, happily married to Amanda, father of Edward and James – aged 10 and 6 respectively, and I live in Sussex (a quiet little village that I'd like to remain so). I've always had the urge to start my own business and since I have been fortunate enough to have had a very good career at GlobalBank as head of sales, UK and US equities, which has brought me financial stability and at least short-term independence, I could fulfil my ambition. At least I could give it a go.

I studied economics and business administration at Greenwood University in the United States. Although not being overly interested in maths, studying economics has helped me to develop an analytical mindset, which means I have a reasonable grasp of financial mathematics. I want to fully understand things and I want them to make sense. I probably find it easier to pick holes in things – find weaknesses, rather than actually exploit them. (I hope I'm on to something here to change that.)

If you know what someone likes and dislikes, you've come a long way towards knowing that person, so I've decided to list a few things I like and dislike.

I like spending time with my family, which is one important reason I decided to go on my own – to give me greater flexibility as to when and how much I work, and to be able to take part in some of the events Edward and James are doing at school, like sports days, concerts and nativities. I like to explore things, try new things. Routine and predictability easily bore me. I enjoy good food and wines. Who doesn't? Beer is my favourite thirst quencher, champagne is second and sometimes mineral water is a must. I have a strong passion for fairness. I don't mind spending money when I get value for money, but when that's not the case, I get seriously upset. I suppose we've started to drift towards the dislikes and I obviously dislike all the opposites to the things I like – like bad food and wine. Jokes aside, I dislike irrationality, which in business more often than not is the result of politics. I hate to lose and to be proved wrong, and I just cannot stand hypocrisy – people who say one thing and do another. I think you know what I mean. I dislike queues and waiting, and I get ants in my pants during meetings with no agenda and meetings that overrun.

As I've already said, this book is about my first steps as an independent fund manager, but what I haven't said is that it's also about derivatives. This is because derivatives are key to my business concept. There are many very good books about derivatives out there, but most of them are highly technical and very few combine the technical stuff with practical experience. I don't think it's necessary to know exactly how to calculate the gamma of an option, but I do believe it's important – even crucial – to understand what derivatives are conceptually, and in this case what the gamma actually tells me about a certain option. I like to know what derivatives can be used for, what factors influence their price and how that price changes as a consequence of changes in one or more of these factors.

Before I started investing other people's money and using derivatives as a tool to enhance portfolio performance, I had to revisit the theory behind derivatives. I took a practical approach and found all that work essential. I'm the first to agree that there's probably no better way of learning than learning from mistakes, your own and other people's. However, it's my strongest wish and hope that this book can teach you things without you having to make too many mistakes yourself. Learn from my mistakes, and also the things I do well.

I hope you find that reading this book actually isn't such a waste of time and money after all.

Good luck and be brave!

Yours sincerely

Thomas R Jones

February 2002

Dear Reader

I don't think anyone knows TR better than I do, so I thought I'd give you a few more hints as to who he really is. TR is a lazy so-and-so. You have to put him under pressure to get things done. Things he can put off till tomorrow, he will. Having said that, he's a doer. I never doubted his commitment to get the new business up and running. I might have doubted he'd do it to his original timetable, but he did. I suppose there was enough in it for him.

It has done him good and I'm very pleased he actually took the opportunity. The boys and I get to see him more, and he's changed. He's more positive and more present when he's with us. Previously his mind was always preoccupied by business issues. I'm not saying that there aren't days or weeks when he's completely consumed by his new business, but I think the fact that he's his own master gives him true satisfaction.

TR is a man of strong views – sometimes on the brink of being outright stubborn – and although he usually avoids confrontation, he doesn't back away from a good discussion or a heated exchange of views.

Before you get to know him, he may come across as a bit cold and closed. But in fact he's the opposite. He's warm, caring, very funny and loving – a bit of a party animal when it comes to that!

I don't understand enough about derivatives to comment on the business concept or the actual business he's running, so I'll leave that up to you.

Love

Amanda

# PROLOGUE

It was early in the morning, as usual. I took the 0615 train to London Bridge and upon arrival I crossed the bridge on foot, which is what I would do every morning. I then walked along King William Street, up past the Bank of England, turned left into Gresham Street and entered the modern office complex that was the European headquarters of GlobalBank. I said hello to Frank at the reception and took the lift to the 15th floor. When I got out of the lift, my daily routine was to change for the first time in 12 years

I didn't bother to go to my desk and switch on the computers and screens. I just walked straight through to Greg Pitcher, my boss for the last three years. Greg was the perfect boss. He didn't just enjoy life up there, but he understood that he had a responsibility to all of us working for him. He knew what he wanted from his staff and he came across as extremely business-minded and focused, but under the skin he was good-hearted. We'd always got on very well with each other. I suppose we were quite close friends within our business environment.

I'd gone over what I was about to say time after time, but I was still nervous. I was pleased I'd made the decision, but leaving a well-paid position would make many people anxious, including me. The upside of course was being able to be my own boss. Maybe more hours would have to be put in at the beginning, but largely I could decide when to do them. It would mean more time with James, Edward and Amanda. But how would Greg react? Would he calmly accept what I told him or would he get emotional and try to talk me into reconsidering my decision?

'Thomas, good morning, have a seat,' said Greg. 'What's on your mind?'

'Well, I don't know quite where to start. I suppose there's no point beating about the bush. You know I've mentioned my dream to start my own business and I've spent the last few months thinking about it more seriously. I've actually written a business plan and started to address all the practical issues involved in starting my own business. It's been hard work to keep up in addition to my work here, but also very rewarding. I'm ready to test my wings.' I was thinking it had gone rather well.

'I hope you're not saying you're leaving GlobalBank. You know how much the mergers and acquisitions guys are relying on us to place their deals. So much is going on. The whole retail sector is reshaping, right. It means good opportunities, big money and you can't just walk away.'

'Greg, please let me continue. There's always going to be another deal – a deal that's bigger, sexier and more profitable. You know, last year's bonus was very generous and I've got enough to go on. I want to take the opportunity now. It's time for a change. My mind's made up. And I'm pretty sure I won't be crawling back on my knees because I've failed.'

'I guess you're right about the bigger, sexier deal around the corner. But have you really thought this through?' asked Greg.

'Yes.'

'So what is it you're going to do?'

'We both know the market for personal wealth is growing exponentially, and although the number of independent fund managers has risen a lot, the big money still goes to the traditional players. I've found quite a few articles and it seems the use of derivatives in fund management is slow to pick up in the UK. The situation in Europe seems to be pretty much the same. The euro offers scope for changes in asset allocation on a pan-European level, within a market and across markets, and derivatives are obviously very useful tools in this respect. I want to start an independent fund management firm. The idea I have is to use derivatives extensively, to be quicker and more flexible than the big firms when it comes to changing exposure.'

'Interesting. Tell me more about it over lunch. I'll sort something out. Right now I've got some business to attend to. See you downstairs at one o'clock. And by the way, since you're not exactly going to a competitor, take a few minutes to say bye to your friends and colleagues. Don't forget to hand in your security pass on the way out.' That was a rather mild treatment. Normally a security officer escorted you to the door. All my personal stuff, I knew, would be sent home by courier.

Greg loved Italian food, and the little restaurant just off the Strand didn't leave any of us disappointed. Over lunch I had the opportunity to reveal my plans in more detail, voice my frustration with traditional fund managers, and explain how I would use derivatives.

The biggest problem I have with traditional fund managers is that they take a relative view. If the other fund managers are losing money, they are happy to lose money, as long as it isn't more than the other guys. When the other guys are making money, they want to show better returns. This is the consequence of blind benchmark tracking, or index tracking. If you're happy to have your money managed that way, by all means do so. But I'm not and I think a growing number of people feel the same. They want someone to actually manage their money for them; to have a view; to use their better understanding of the financial markets to formulate an investment strategy for that particular fund. There is no incentive for traditional fund managers to use derivatives to try to lose less than other fund managers, because if the market goes up, they will underperform compared to the others. That's probably one reason why fund managers in Europe are not using derivatives to any great extent.

My idea is to use derivatives, not to curtail performance but to improve it. By using options in various ways, I can increase and reduce exposure, taking advantage of dull or seriously volatile markets.

# CHAPTER ONE

## 22 March 2000

A month after I resigned from GlobalBank I was about to have my first board meeting in the new company. The board meeting was going to be the sweetest moment in my entire professional career. All the anxiety of leaving a well-paid position at GlobalBank, the doubts over whether I could do something like this on my own, the joy as pieces started to fall into place and the growing self-confidence as I began to set up my own company, they were finally going to be tested at the first meeting of the board. Not for a second did I believe the board would overturn a good project for the sake of it, but I knew that they were all highly regarded and professional in their approach. They wouldn't want to give the go-ahead unless all the loose ends had been tied up. I'm in the process of obtaining regulatory approval and the financial situation looks good – I'll manage two years without any business coming in. Unlikely and hopefully not true.

During the last week I've been working on the agenda and what to send out in advance of the meeting. There are several things to discuss – current status of the company, our application to become a regulated investment company, finances and probably the most important, how the business is going to be run. I have some catching up to do in terms of derivatives to make sure I understand as much as I need to. This means consulting my old textbooks and any new works that can shed light on the subject. I've drafted the proposed investment strategy of Fund1, which will be a good test of my current thinking. This is the final pack to be sent out.

The investment strategy is important, because it needs to allow

**BOARD MEETING**
**01-28/03/00**
**AGENDA**

| | | |
|---|---|---|
| 1. | Introductions | BS/ALL |
| 2. | Update | TR |
| | – Overall progress | |
| | – Regulatory issues | |
| | – Derivatives work to be done | |
| | – Marketing campaign | DM/TR |
| 3. | Financial situation | TR |
| 4. | Draft investment strategy Fund1 | TR |
| 5. | AOB | BS/ALL |

Attachments: List of board members
Proposed investment strategy Fund1

**LIST OF BOARD MEMBERS**

Prof. Benjamin Saunders (board chairman)
Greenwood University
Mr Greg Pitcher
Managing Director, GlobalBank
Mr Simon H Collins
Director, Euro Derivatives Exchange
Mr Donald MacLean
CEO, Lighthouse Advertising Agency
Mr Thomas R Jones
CEO and Compliance Officer, TRJI Ltd

Accountant
Mr Tim Burrows Bright, Smith & Lourdes Partnership

**PROPOSED INVESTMENT STRATEGY FOR FUND1**

**Scope**
UK equities with an outlook to provide investment opportunities in growth companies and markets in Europe.

**Investment strategy**
**UK equities** – minimum 80% of fund value, maximum 95% of fund value
**Other European equities** – minimum 0% of fund value, maximum 15% of fund value
So that 95% of fund value is always invested in equities
**Cash or equity derivatives** – 5% of fund value

**Further definitions**
**Base portfolio**
95% UK equities and 5% cash
UK equities allocated to sectors in the following proportions (totalling 100% of 95%):
25% Telecom
15% Retail
20% Banking/finance
15% Property
25% Other
The base portfolio should have a historical correlation – over the last two years – with the Market100 index of at least 90%.

**Derivatives**
Derivatives can be used to hedge the value of the portfolio when a decline in the market is expected. Derivatives can also be used to enhance portfolio value during other market conditions. However, derivatives premiums may never exceed 5% of the total portfolio value. Short positions allow greater exposure, but at any given time, no derivatives position may risk more than 10% of the fund value.

**Benchmark**
Fund1 will be measured against the Market100 index. Maximum underperformance at any given moment is 15%. At an underperformance of 10% the portfolio should revert back to the base portfolio.

the flexibility to use derivatives and to capture opportunities in fast-growing companies in the UK as well as in the rest of Europe. At the same time, it must ensure a significant closeness to the benchmark, Market100. At the moment, I can't say whether I've got it perfect, but I'm sure by the time I start to invest it will be. Most definitely, the board will want to be absolutely certain the strategy ties in well with the overall approach to risk and risk management before giving the final go-ahead.

The strategy introduces a few risks, which I'll have to understand fully and be able to monitor and manage. By allowing investments in countries other than the UK, I'll expose myself to currency risk. Another risk is the potential exposure to companies outside of Market100 constituents. The third and most significant risk is the added complexity of the market risk through the use of derivatives.

**Back to preparations for the board meeting**

The board members are all excellent. Not only are they close friends of mine, but their respective professional skills and careers should be very useful in developing the company. They'll give credibility to the business and their networks will surely bring a stream of clients. My worry is that should something go pear-shaped, we might cease to be friends, but you never know. Anyhow, I wouldn't want to change things. This is the perfect board.

Professor Saunders is a great academic. I met him for the first time when I studied at Greenwood University and I've met him on a number of occasions since then. Professor Saunders, or Ben as I call him, has a top-notch reputation. For the past 15 years he's been at the forefront of research into state-of-the-art pricing and valuation models for the financial markets, particularly the derivatives market. Few in the academic world or indeed in the financial industry would be surprised if he received the Nobel Prize.

Over the years we've become really good friends. Ben's jovial, charming and very interesting to be with. He's been increasingly in demand as a keynote speaker at seminars and conferences around the world, which means he's always got a lot to talk about. What I value the most is his wealth of experience in the financial markets and the derivatives markets in particular. He can turn his theoretical knowledge into practical experience, and he knows pretty much everyone worth knowing in the industry, so he's heard all the anecdotes – the success stories and the failures.

Five years have passed since I chaired the third Derivatives Congress, to which Ben was invited as a keynote speaker. On the opening night, we had dinner at the Imperial City, underneath the Royal Exchange opposite the Bank of England. We had plenty to catch up on, but I most strongly remember discussing with him my career options. It was really the first time we'd touched upon the subject. In fact, it was the first time I'd discussed my career with anyone.

I had three options. I could stay with GlobalBank, where I'd already worked nearly seven years. I could join my father in the family business to learn the tricks of the trade, but I never really saw that as the way to go. I was rather hoping Steven, my younger brother, would assume that responsibility. Unfortunately, he never showed much interest in anything to do with business or money, other than spending it on a lavish lifestyle. Or I could start my own business; that was my strongest inclination.

I was spurred by Adam, one of my closest friends, who together with three of his friends from Oxford, decided to start a company in the field of public relations. It seemed obvious to me they would succeed – they chose the right field, planned the business to perfection, worked hard and complemented each other very well. I've always struggled to come up with the right business idea or indeed suss out whether I should go it alone or with partners. I remember Ben strongly recommended that I should pursue my career at GlobalBank. He wanted me to take a long-term view and stressed the importance of building a strong financial platform from which I could later set out to conquer the world, as he put it. I knew he was right, so I stayed with Global-Bank, until now, that is.

Ben always stresses that you should do your homework before getting down to business. Here is one of his favourite homework stories. One summer, in the mid-1980s, a trader/speculator thought the price of the potato contract was high, bearing in mind that the crop forecasts looked really good. So he started to sell the contract. He kept selling for nearly three weeks and the price drifted lower and lower, but suddenly, towards the end of the third week, another trader started to buy and he bought more contracts than the first trader was selling. Soon the whole market was buying. Prices rocketed and the poor trader who started all the selling couldn't believe his eyes. What was going on? He had to start buying contracts to cover his by then very short position.

He asked around in the market in order to find out why people were buying so heavily. Looking at the current market price and the prediction about the crop, he was dead right. He learnt that only Idaho potatoes were deliverable against the contract and that his short position was at one stage larger than the whole market. That clearly triggered speculative buying and our poor friend had to cover his short position at a greater and greater loss. I am sad to say, he didn't last very much longer in the market than the expiry date of that contract. Lesson to learn: always make sure you understand the contract, what is deliverable, how settlement prices are calculated and, more obviously, when the contract settles.

Another story I remember quite well is the one about a German corporate treasurer, who used derivatives to counter a sharp fall in the value of the Swedish krona. Early in 1992 the corporate treasurer of a German manufacturing company with substantial sales to the Swedish market was worried that the value of the Swedish krona would depreciate substantially and seriously hurt the revenue from the sales to the Swedish market. At that time the krona was pegged against a trade-weighted basket of currencies and so far the central bank had managed to keep the currency within its band. There was a strong commitment to this regime, just as there was in the UK up until Black Wednesday, when the pound was forced out of the ERM.

Anyway, the corporate treasurer thought of various ways to protect himself from the advent of a fall in the krona. After serious consideration, he decided to follow the advice to buy krona–Deutschmark put options – options that gave him the right to sell krona at a given level against the Deutschmark. In September 1992 the Swedish central bank had to give up the defence of the krona and the currency started to float with an initial fall in value against the Deutschmark of around 30%. The corporate treasurer's action actually led to higher sales revenue year-on-year against all expectations.

Ben also had stories on pitfalls and unfortunate outcomes. Here's one of them. On the notion that timing is everything, in 1987, before the stock market crash, a trader, who thought himself to be bigger than big, correctly predicted that the market would fall. He started to accumulate, through derivatives, a short position in the September contract. It was a massive position of long put options, short call options, and short futures contracts – the lot. Massive enough to put the firm out of business, which it did, because the fact of the matter was that the stock market was going up and the September contracts closed higher, incurring phenomenal losses. Then, as we all know, in October the market crashed. Mr Big was right about the crash, but his timing was devastating.

A few weeks ago I had made arrangements to meet Tim, my new accountant, for a meeting at IMRO, which is short for Investment Management Regulatory Organisation. We had made an appointment to find out where in the process our application was. Tim is prudence personified. I don't think I would have made it this far without him. He knows all there is to know about setting up companies, taxes and how to do things in the most efficient way.

Tim's office was situated in Bartholomew Close, just behind Smithfield Market. It was very well secluded – almost like a small town in itself – and still more or less in the middle of the City. Tim had good news. The company, Thomas R Jones Investments Ltd, was up and running. After some discussion we agreed to keep the name that way. I considered Jones Investments Ltd, the TRJ Investment Company Ltd, TRJ Investments Ltd and TRJ Global Fund Management Ltd, but Thomas R Jones Investments Ltd it was. It sounded more personal and that's the impression I wanted.

After a quick sandwich and a pint at my favourite pub, Ryan's Bar off Ludgate Hill, we made our way to Canary Wharf, where IMRO is located.

IMRO is a self-regulating organisation; its purpose is to protect investors by regulating those who manage the investments of others. Currently, IMRO has about 1200 regulated firms, of which fund managers are in one category. To obtain IMRO regulated status, a firm must establish systems or ways of ensuring observance of the IMRO rules and for reporting to IMRO. The firm will have to cooperate with any request for information or any investigation by IMRO, and it must accept IMRO's disciplinary system. More importantly, the firm must prove to the Admissions Committee that it is and will remain 'fit and proper' to carry out the investment business it proposes. As a member you're paying an annual subscription fee, based on funds under management and gross income. The process of obtaining approval normally takes about 12 weeks, but since we were already in the process, they estimated it would take another three to four weeks before we had it.

Donald MacLean is CEO, founder, owner and inspirational guru of Lighthouse Advertising Agency. I met him around three years ago. From the first meeting there was something I liked about him. Don started his own business and has been very successful, but he has never let success go to his head. He is generous and generally extremely relaxed. At the same time though, he has the quality of quickly understanding the challenge at hand. Creative and commercially focused, he nearly always came up with the bones of a good idea, and quickly too – he knew how to package and make campaigns work. I haven't really tapped into his experience of starting a business, but I will. For the board meeting I've asked him to present an embryo of a marketing campaign. That's our little surprise.

Simon Collins, director at Euro Derivatives Exchange, knows all there is to know about exchange-traded derivatives. He has been with the exchange for nearly 12 years and seems to be thrilled to bits by the idea of joining the board. I don't think he is fully stretched at what he is doing. I mean there are only so many contracts or products you can successfully introduce and trade on exchange. The markets like transparency to a certain degree, but not across the board. They want some benchmarks from which they can price other instruments, with maintained flexibility to add their own spin and without having the transparency that follows exchange-traded contracts. Simon is a nice guy, but a bit difficult to really get to know. Of all the board members, I'd say our relationship is the least personal. However, since most of the derivatives trading I'll be doing will be on exchange, I expect him to provide lots of useful information on how futures and options work, how I can access the market and everything else there is to know about exchange-traded derivatives.

Finally, Greg Pitcher, my former boss at GlobalBank, who I've already mentioned, is probably the best salesperson I've ever come across. He is never offensive and he knows when to push or call it a day. He makes people feel so relaxed that they buy into pretty much all he is saying. 'Networking – get to know your client, what makes him tick, and get involved. Take him to an evening of mud-wrestling if that's what he wants.' Greg's philosophy in a nutshell. This quality is renowned within GlobalBank and the key factor in his rapid move up the career ladder.

## 28 March 2000

Big day. Board meeting day. I am renting an office in Albemarle Street. Not the biggest or most luxurious of offices, but for the time being perfect for Caroline and me. Caroline Parkin is my assistant. An Oxford graduate, she's very bright and I think she'll be very useful when it comes to actual business and dealing with clients. Now, understandably, her work is more of a PA to me. When I have my down days, she's a very good reason to make it into the office. She is funny, witty and sometimes quite sarcastic. Although young, she's got strong opinions and is very well organised. Being just the two of us, I feel the responsibility of helping her to settle in and giving a good start to her career.

I'd decided to hold the meeting away from the office, at the Stafford, which is fairly nearby. Handy, since I wanted us all to go back to the office after the meeting for a little surprise – officially open the office, cut the ribbon and all that, followed by a buffet lunch. Caroline, with help from Amanda, was left to organise that. I took care of the board meeting.

Almost an hour before the meeting was due to start, I entered the meeting room to make sure tea and coffee were in place. I relaxed, sat down and let my mind drift. It felt like I'd been there for ages when Ben arrived.

Greg was next, shortly followed by Simon. The three of them seemed to get along well together. That was a relief. Ten minutes later Don was there, just as Ben was about to start the meeting. Marvellous, we could begin. I've included the minutes for you to see.

Back at the office Ben cut the ribbon and officially launched the company, Thomas R Jones Investments Limited. 'Champagne,' I cried out loudly, and we all dug in. It was a serious do. I think everyone had a good time. Not much work done by anyone involved that afternoon. Amanda and I left last at 10pm. We got home then cracked open another bottle of C. Put up a good show, I think. I'd done everything in my power to please everyone. What a day!

**BOARD MEETING MINUTES 28/03/00**

ATTENDEES:
BEN SAUNDERS (BS)
GREG PITCHER (GP)
DON McLEAN (DM)
SIMON COLLINS (SC)
TIM BURROWS (TB)
THOMAS JONES (TR )

APOLOGIES:
NONE

Time of the meeting: 10am to 1pm

1. **Introduction**
   - BS opened the meeting and introduced all board members.
   - BS presented the agenda. Agenda agreed without amendments.
2. **Update**

   TR reported on progress and particularly the following items:

   **Overall progress**
   - The company, Thomas R Jones Investments is now a registered limited company.
   - Planned go-live date is 14 December 2000.
   - An office has been rented in Albemarle Street for the next 24 months. TR invited everyone back there to a buffet luncheon after the meeting.
   - TR introduced CP, his assistant, who all would meet at the luncheon.

   **Regulatory issues**

   IMRO registration – TR and TB visited IMRO last week. Approved status likely to be given within the next three to four weeks.

   **Derivatives work to be undertaken**

   Basic overview including:

   Calls and puts
   Different types of options – European and American
   Buying vs writing options
   The Greeks
   Exchange-traded derivatives
   Black–Scholes model and other models
   Basic relationships between futures and options
   Put/call parity

Risk measurement management
Some basic options strategies

**Marketing campaign**

DM presented an embryonic marketing campaign, which will be launched in November/December during the run-up to the actual go-live date. It focuses on superior performance in bad times as well as the readiness to take new opportunities leading to enhanced portfolio performance, even in good times. The target audience was described as anyone who wanted a bit more out of their invested funds than simply index tracking. The board agreed the style was along the right lines and that the target audience had to be firmed up.

3. **Financial situation**

TR discussed the financial situation. So far, less expenditure than expected. The company will manage about two years without significant business developing. (However, it would be a disaster for TR personally.)

4. **Draft investment strategy for Fund1**

TR introduced the draft investment strategy for Fund1 (see page 11). GP suggested the strategy be revisited when the above-mentioned derivatives work had been concluded. All agreed.

5. **AOB**

**Board member remuneration**

TR suggested either cash or equity in the company. Cash in the short term would put pressure on the cash flow. Equity would not impact the cash flow short-term. Also discussed which option may ensure best involvement and commitment. DM suggested equity. Success would rub off on the board members.

Stressed board member stake should not exceed 30%. GP advocated second option, but suggested postponement of final decision to next meeting. GP would contribute some possible alternative under the equity route. All agreed to postpone decision to next meeting.

**Next meeting**

Next meeting to be held 14 December 2000 at 11.00am, The Stafford.

TR invited all to luncheon at the TRJI Ltd new office.

BS thanked all and closed the meeting.

## 29 March 2000

What a morning! Felt awful. I wasn't alone. Amanda was suffering enormously as well. Heads or tails and I lost. Had to take the boys to school.

The journey into work was more horrendous than ever. When I arrived I found Caroline up to her armpits in debris from the day before. I took her to lunch and after a few glasses of wine, we both felt better. I asked her to sort out some cleaners and then she could have the rest of the day off. I carried on in grand style at the City Club, where Tony is a member. Kindly invited me to spend the afternoon there. Thoughtful, very thoughtful.

Tony Clarke had become a very good friend of mine. The fact that we used to travel home on the same train, more or less every day, meant we met up at least once a week for a quick pint before getting on the train. Now we just carried on from the club. Occasionally, we got stuck in some sort of discussion and one pint followed another. Today was such a day. We missed two trains before I phoned Amanda to say I'd be late. She wasn't very happy and shouted back: I'd promised to be home early, I'd promised to spend more time with the boys until the business picked up and I would have to make my own dinner when I got home.

I turned to face Tony to say I probably had to be off soon, but he was gone. I looked around and found him at the bar, buying another round. He told me he wanted to get some things off his chest. Apparently, his bank had merged with a German bank and that was the cause of his anger. I'm glad I'm out of it, and even more convinced I made the right decision to leave the rat race at GlobalBank.

## 10 April 2000

So here I am. Time to dig into the world of derivatives. I lined up my textbooks and began to flick through them. 'Introduction' seemed like a good place to start. Just then, Caroline entered the room and asked what derivatives were all about: 'If I'm going to work here, I would like to know what derivatives are. I believe they're the key to our investment strategy.'

'Very well! Since I'm just about to refresh my own understanding of derivatives, my explaining to you might actually be a good way of doing it. Let me have half an hour to prepare then I'll give you a first basic run-through.'

A short time later we began. 'In the market, "derivatives" is the brand name for contracts – typically futures and options – which are based on the price of an underlying commodity. The commodity in question could be anything from pork bellies to government bonds. A futures contract is an agreement to buy or indeed sell the underlying commodity, at a given time in the future, at a price determined and agreed today.

'This is important to remember, because it is one of the distinguishing factors between futures and options in the sense that a futures contract only has a single price at any given moment (ignoring the bid–offer spread; that's the difference between the price you can sell at and the price you can buy at), whereas an option contract has a number of different tradeable prices, depending on the strike price.

'The strike price is the price in the future – when the contract expires – you've agreed to buy or sell the underlying commodity at. Theoretically, the futures price should equal the current market price for the commodity plus the cost of carry, which is the interest that would be incurred when buying the underlying commodity today, and it is kept to the expiry date of the contract.

'This means profits and losses from the futures contract pretty much go hand in hand with profits and losses in the cash market for the commodity, disregarding the cost of money. With options, however, this is different. If you buy an options contract – call or put – your profits can soar, but your losses will never exceed the premium – that is what you paid for the contract. Sounds like a good idea to me, don't you think?'

'So far I'm with you.'

'Fine, with a futures contract you're obliged to buy or sell the underlying commodity, whereas with options you have the right, but not the obligation, to do just that. I mean, if you bought a call option with a strike price or target price of £10, giving you the right to buy the underlying commodity for £10, you would only exercise that right if the price of the commodity was equal to or higher than £10. If the price of the commodity was £5, whatever you paid for the contract would be lost and instead of making an unwise decision to exercise your right to buy at £10, you would rather buy the commodity in the market for £5.

'Options contracts that are trading or closing at a higher price than the strike price are called "in the money" options. Options trading or closing at a price that's the same as the strike price are called "at the money" options, and you've probably guessed that options trading or closing at a price below the strike price are called "out of the money" options.'

'No I didn't guess, but I think I see what you mean.'

'Okay, have a look at this diagram of a long call option. Perhaps it'll make things clearer. You see that the option will have to close slightly higher than the strike price to break even. That is to actually recoup the premium paid for the call option.'

'Fine, but how do I trade these things looking like ice-hockey sticks?'

'Well, derivatives are either traded on an exchange or off exchange. Off-exchange trading is called over-the-counter trading or OTC trading. Without going into too much detail, exchange-traded derivatives are traded on an exchange – the market – which is regulated and organised in a way to provide a well-functioning price mechanism. Many buyers and sellers access the market on an ongoing basis, and prices and trades are disclosed to the market immediately. Exchange-traded derivatives must be highly standardised to attract enough interest to warrant a central marketplace.

'OTC derivatives are normally not standardised, but rather tailor-made to better meet the needs of a market participant,

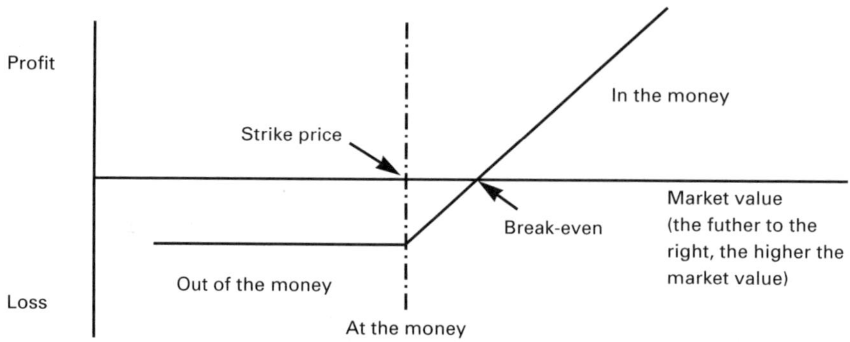


**Profit and loss diagram of a long call option**

meaning that OTC derivatives are "negotiated" between two parties. On an ongoing basis it is "easier" to enter into and close exchange-traded derivatives positions than positions taken in OTC derivatives. So, Caroline, what do you think so far?'

'I think I follow what you've said so far, but I still haven't grasped who would use derivatives. Could you give me a few examples?'

'Of course. Typical users of derivatives are traders, portfolio managers, borrowers, lenders, manufacturers, speculators and arbitrageurs. Traders are probably the most versatile users, since they use them for trading, speculation, hedging and arbitrage. Others, like manufacturers, are mostly in it for hedging. I would think fund managers are closer to traders than manufacturers.

'The simple use of derivatives for a manufacturer or a farmer would be to use outright contracts to "lock in" future prices of, for example, raw materials needed in production or, in the case of the farmer, the crop he is expecting. The manufacturer could buy (long) futures contracts or buy call options to lock in a future price, since he would have to buy raw materials in the future. The farmer, however, wants to sell his "product" in the future, so he will either sell (short) futures contracts or buy put options, which will give him the right, but not the obligation, to sell at a given price.

'When it comes to speculating, derivatives offer tremendous opportunities, but also tremendous risks. The name of the game is leverage. The whole idea is that you don't have to worry about financing or what to do with a pile of cash (if you're selling assets), because that issue is deferred to the settlement day of the contract in question – could be three months or three years away, depending on market practice. The only thing you have to pay is a margin.

'The margin is used to cover potential losses during the life of the contract. This means that for a relatively small sum of money a much bigger position in exposure terms could be established than in the cash market. However, if losses accumulate and grow beyond the initial margin, additional margin will be called and, depending on the contract and the adverse market movement, this could be substantial money.

'Most of the scandals I've read or heard about have all been by people "speculating" with other people's money, be it banks', firms' or pension savers' money. Greed, or rather self-deception, in combination with the lack of control systems and an understanding of the risks involved by senior management are the causes of these scandals.' I finished. Caroline seemed pleased with that for the time being. I gave her some literature to read, which I gathered would keep her busy for some time.

That was a flying start. But I needed to speed up my own refresher course and I decided to move on to arbitrage, after a cup of tea.

Back at the drawing board, the books explained arbitrage as a way of making money without taking risks. It is all about exploiting inefficiencies in the market. For example, some financial instruments have strict relationships with others and when they fall out of that 'ideal' relationship there is an opportunity for arbitrage. In terms of options, this is called the put/call parity. By combining a short call and a long put at the same strike with the same expiry date, you synthetically create a short position in the underlying, so by buying the underlying at the same time, a risk-free position is established. Now, if this can be done at a profit, arbitrage exists and arbitrageurs will flood the market and their activity will inevitably re-establish the put/call parity.

Assuming an unchanged price in the underlying, the price of the put option must equal the price of the call option; that is, what I receive by selling a call must equal what I'll have to pay for the long put option, otherwise arbitrage exists. The theory is true only for European options and 'requires' us to ignore the time value of money – financing cost and opportunity cost – and transaction costs. The opportunities are normally small and short-lived, and to make it worthwhile they require large positions to be taken. It also requires direct access to the markets, so I guess it is a game for the professional players like investment banks or hedge funds. Maybe I'll have a shout at it!

Futures, I suppose, are not too different from forwards, that is, contracts to buy or sell with a settlement time beyond the normal settlement cycle. The main difference is that futures are traded on exchange and forwards normally not. In most cash markets a normal settlement cycle is three to five days, meaning that if I buy shares today, I will have to pay for them upon delivery, three to five days from now. The forward market will allow me to postpone payment for the shares to a future date, let's say three months from now. If, two weeks later, I decide to sell the shares I bought in the forward market, the common practice is to settle a new forward contract three months from that date. Unless I can negotiate someone to buy the shares from me within two and a half months, I will end up having a mismatch of two weeks, which means that when the first forward contract expires, I will have to pay for the shares and keep them for two weeks, and then sell according to the second forward contract.

The problem I'm facing in this situation is the fact that I'll have to finance the purchase for two weeks. If I haven't got the cash, I'll have to borrow. For me to break even, the profit over the two-week holding period will have to make up for the cost of carry, that is, the financing cost over the weeks.

If I traded actively, I would end up having lots of loose ends and, potentially, significant funding requirements. This is where I believe futures and options, at least exchange-traded futures and options, add value. Through the life of these derivatives you can buy and sell contracts with the same delivery dates, which offset any funding requirements due to mismatches in trading positions. This is the key. I need to know more about what distinguishes exchange-traded contracts from forward contracts. Moreover, as I buy and sell contracts, I believe I only have to pay margin on the net position. I'll call Simon at the Euro Derivatives Exchange to get this clarified.

Options are clearly more complex than futures, so I'd better go over some of the basics again. First of all there are two types of options – calls and puts. Calls give you the right to buy the underlying commodity, whereas puts give you the right to sell the underlying commodity. So by buying calls or puts you'll get the right – but not the obligation – to buy or sell the underlying. For me to be able to buy these options, someone must be on the other side and write the options. The writer of an option has the obligation to honour exercise if the buyer of the option wishes to do so. The buyer normally pays a premium, which the writer of the option receives – that is his compensation. Coffee, I need coffee. Luckily there was a coffee shop in the street next to the office and although I could have asked Caroline to pop down, I found out what she wanted and went along myself. I needed some fresh air.

Next I had to confirm my understanding of the different types of options. There are European, American, Bermudan and Asian style options. Bermudan and Asian are only of academic value to know about. The important ones are European and American. Nevertheless, the key differentiating point is how and when the options can be exercised. European-style options can only be exercised on the expiry day and at the settlement price. This means that, for example, only calls in the money will be exercised. (Unless there is a significant demand for the underlying, which could lead to at the money and even out of the money options being exercised. This would only happen if the underlying could be obtained at a lower price than in the market; for example, if the idea is to buy a lot of the underlying, then that activity in the cash market will push the market up and consequently, some out of the money options may be worthwhile exercising.)

I can obviously get rid of my options, prior to expiry, by selling them. But hang on, I must clarify the terminology. When I buy an option it is called 'opening purchase' and when I want to close that position I do a 'closing sale'. The writer of an option does an 'opening sale' and when he closes it, it's called a 'closing purchase'. It's important to remember this, because in some books they use 'sell' synonymously with 'write'. And more important, I must make it crystal clear what I want to do when talking to my broker, otherwise I may end up writing an option rather than closing my original trade.

American options can be exercised at any time during their life, and Bermudan options are in between European and American options insofar as they can be exercised before expiry, but only at predefined times, for example every Wednesday, prior to expiry. European, American and Bermudan options expire at a given price, which is normally the current market price at that time. Asian options, however, expire at an average price of the underlying, which is calculated over a given period of time.

Next I decided to take a closer look at the Greeks, as they're known in the textbooks. I've never really liked too much maths and technical stuff, but I fear I need to have a basic understanding of the Greeks. They're really just measures of one or more options' sensitivity to certain features. Delta measures the sensitivity to the underlying asset (changes in the price of it). Gamma measures the sensitivity in the delta, which is a useful measure when keeping a delta-neutral position. A delta-neutral position is a position where a change in the price of the underlying asset is fully offset by the change in value of the option(s) in the position. A high gamma means that I will have to rebalance quite frequently, because with a change in the price of the underlying, the value of the delta for my options will change more, consequently the position isn't delta-neutral anymore. Theta measures the sensitivity to time. Over time the value of an option with a high theta will decay more rapidly than the value of an option with a lower theta.

Then we have rho, which is a measure of the sensitivity to the interest rate in the Black–Scholes formula. Incidentally, this is the formula most widely used for options calculations – the market standard. Finally, vega is a measure of the sensitivity to volatility. Volatility in its turn is a measure of the movements in the price of the underlying asset. Low volatility means movements in the asset price are small and infrequent, whereas high volatility means price movements are frequent and bigger. It is difficult to know the volatility exactly, and different players make their own calculations, hence there is scope for trading. When the price of an option is given, the implied volatility can be calculated. Consequently, the implied volatility is a measure of the market's view on the volatility at a given price for an option.

| | **Delta** | **Gamma** | **Theta** | **Vega** |
|---|---|---|---|---|
| Out of the money | low | low | low | medium |
| At the money | medium | high | high | high |
| In the money | high | low | low | medium |

The table above is a summary for a call option. It indicates that delta, the proportion by which the call option changes in value in relation to the underlying's change in value, is low for out of the money options. Delta increases as the option moves to at the money or in the money. Gamma, which measures the change in the delta, is highest for at the money. Theta, the sensitivity to time, and vega, the sensitivity to volatility, are also highest for at the money calls. That'll do for now.

## 13 April 2000

Contacted Simon for a 'lecture' on exchange-traded derivatives. We always have a good time and this one was no different. Simon had come across what was allegedly one of the oldest wine bars in London. It was situated on the south side of London Bridge. Not only was it difficult to find the way there, but the amount of wine made it nearly as difficult to find the way back. Anyway, it was a very useful meeting. My notes look quite good and I think we managed to cover most of the basics before the drinking got serious. We had a few bottles of a very good Lebanese wine, Château Musar. Must remember that.

First we spoke about definitions. Simon presented a contract specification, which was really useful to discuss. We then covered how I can actually trade. In order to start trading, I have to open an account with a broker who is prepared to take on new clients. My broker could be my bank or a firm that specialises in executing client business on one or many exchanges. Next I must consider the level of service I want from the broker. The most common are execution-only, advisory and discretionary. Execution-only is obvious. It means the broker accesses the market to buy or sell on your behalf, and that's it. Advisory implies I can get suggestions on when and what to do. Discretionary is not for me, because that is what I'm supposed to be doing, but it means that a sum of capital is handed over to the broker for him to invest on behalf of the client. Execution-only is the least expensive service.

When I give my broker an order, I must specify which contract I wish to deal in, whether it's a call or a put, whether I wish to buy or sell, how many contracts I wish to buy or sell, the relevant contract terms (for options this is the expiry month and the exercise price), whether I'm opening a new position or closing an existing one, and what price I'm prepared to deal at. The broker will deduct premiums, margins and other trading costs from my account, probably the day after I've traded. I'll then receive a trade confirmation from the broker specifying the trade details, such as what I bought or sold, the price at which I bought or sold and, unfortunately, the broker's commission charges. There are no free lunches.

Next we discussed margins. (By the way, this is when the first bottle of Ch. Musar arrived.) Margin is the amount of collateral

**TYPICAL CONTRACT SPECIFICATION**

**Market100 index option (American style)**
**Unit of trading**
Valued at £10 per index point
(e.g. value £1000 at 100)

**Expiry months**
March, June, September and December, plus additional months such that the three nearest calendar months are always available for trading

**Exercise/settlement day**
Exercise by 1615 on any business day. Settlement is the first business after the day of exercise/the last trading day

**Expiry time and day**
1100
Third Friday in the expiry month

**Quotation**
Index points

**Minimum price movement**
0.5 index point

**Tick value**
£5.00

**Trading hours**
0800–1600

that buyers or sellers of futures contracts and writers of options contracts are required to deposit with their brokers as security for performance of their obligations. The buyer of a long options contract will sometimes pay the premium and sometimes just provide a margin. However, in this case the maximum loss is known and additional margin will not be required. Margin payments may be satisfied by collateral, deposited in the form of cash, or they could be provided in a wide variety of other forms, including the asset underlying the relevant contract. The broker will advise on the types of collateral he is willing to accept. The amount of margin required is fundamentally determined by the exchange or rather the clearing house. Margin requirements are recalculated on a daily basis, in accordance with the movement of the underlying market price. To avoid frequent changes in the amount of collateral provided, many brokers require their clients to lodge collateral in excess of a minimum figure and insist that sufficient collateral is in place to cover margin requirements before clients open positions.

Finally, Simon gave a brilliant little 'speech' on why I should trade 'on exchange' and what they actually do to enlighten people like myself. Transparency, liquidity and rules providing best execution were the key points he made. Transparency relates to the information that the general public or 'investment community' receive from the market on an immediate and ongoing basis. Prices and number of traded contracts (volume) are the important pieces of information. Liquidity is an indicator of how efficient the market is. The tighter the bid–offer spread, the greater the liquidity. The easier to buy or sell large positions, the better the liquidity. And the more liquid a contract, the higher the turnover.

Before we wound up, he did mention their website. Should visit that soon.

# CHAPTER TWO

## 3 May 2000

First of all, good news. The regulatory approval has come through. I called Ben and Tim and they joined in the cheering.

Anyway, at the first Derivatives Congress some years ago I picked up an 'options calculator' in CD-ROM format, which I at last will have the benefit of using.

| Settings | Values | Greeks | Call results | Put results |
|---|---|---|---|---|
| Market price | 99 | Call/put | 1.9892 | 2.0756 |
| Strike price | 100 | Delta | 0.5035 | 20.4965 |
| Volatility | 12 | Gamma | 0.0784 | 0.0784 |
| Interest rate | 5 | Rho | 0.0878 | 20.0940 |
| Days left | 67 | Theta | 20.0217 | 20.0081 |
| | | Vega | 0.16920 | 0.1692 |
| | | Implied vol. | 12.6543 | 13.0301 |

I must say, it took quite some time to understand how to use it. After some serious thinking and consultation with Simon, I felt confident to go ahead. This is going to be an awesome maths session. The formula it uses seems to be the Black–Scholes, European, which is the most appropriate for calculating index options generally and Market100 specifically. It provides a number of other formulas too, but this one rings a bell, so I'll stick to it.

One of the key benefits of derivatives is the possibility to protect the portfolio from declining share prices in any market where derivatives are available. There are several ways to protect your portfolio value or at least to limit the impact of falling markets, but my aim is to prove to myself that derivatives, or rather options, which will be my focus in my actual fund management, are superior to other strategies. Here are the four strategies I will explore:

- I don't do anything.
- I sell part of the portfolio (500 units) and hold cash instead.
- I rebalance the portfolio to reduce 'correlation' or sensitivity to market changes.
- I buy put options on market index (benchmark).

If I'm brave enough, I may even try some options strategies. I will try to work through each of these strategies to determine the outcomes. For this exercise I will assume I have a fund total of £1 000 000, of which 95% is invested in Market100 constituents, replicating the index to 100%. Let's assume the current value of Market100 is 100. So £950 000 is invested in shares (I have 9500 units of Market100) and £50 000 is held in cash. The interest rate for cash is 5% annually, so I will earn 5% interest on the cash I hold during one year. This exercise will look at changes in portfolio value over a period of 30 days with time to options expiry being 45 days at the outset, and when I do the re-evaluation of the portfolio, the options will have 15 days left to expiry. Volatility is 12% in all these examples. Let's assume two different outcomes: the first where the market falls by 3% and the second where the market falls by 7%. On day 1, in all alternatives, I have a total value of £1 000 000, of which £950 000 is invested in Market100 and the remaining £50 000 is held in cash (or used for derivatives). After 30 days this is the outcome using the different strategies.

Let's start with the do-nothing strategy. Some strategy, hey, but I've seen it in practice many times. If you haven't done anything, you can't be blamed for it. I suppose you could call it the Ostrich strategy, after the big bird that sticks its head in the sand. You're rarely punished for missed opportunities; I hope I can prove them wrong.

| I don't do anything | £ |
|---|---|
| Fund value at the beginning | 950 000 |
| Cash value at the beginning | 50 000 |
| Total value at the beginning | 1 000 000 |
| MARKET CHANGE after 30 days | −3% |
| New fund value | 921 500 |
| New cash value | 50 208 |
| New total value | 971 708 |
| TOTAL VALUE CHANGE | −28 292 |
| PERCENT VALUE CHANGE | −2.83% |

Anyway, the outcome wasn't all that difficult to predict. Since I had £50 000 in cash, the net result had to be less than −3%. I suppose the fall in portfolio value will be slightly less than 7% in the second scenario, so let's see.

| I don't do anything | £ |
|---|---|
| Fund value at the beginning | 950 000 |
| Cash value at the beginning | 50 000 |
| Total value at the beginning | 1 000 000 |
| MARKET CHANGE after 30 days | −7% |
| New fund value | 883 500 |
| New cash value | 50 208 |
| New total value | 933 708 |
| TOTAL VALUE CHANGE | −66 292 |
| PERCENT VALUE CHANGE | −6.63% |

Yes, confirmed. −6.63%. I need a break.

I came to think about a nutty professor that I once met, who said he could calculate the premium of an option in his head. When looking at an options pricing formula it looks like an insurmountable task. I think he had some shortcut or abbreviation to it all, including volatility, the vega and the square root of the number of days remaining. By multiplying these you should arrive at the price in percent. I fiddled around with the options calculator and eventually got a result in the right ballpark. However, there was no way I could verify the result. I don't even know if I got the formula right. Normally, I don't bother remembering things like this, but it was such a unique statement that in a sense I just had to remember it. I scribbled it down on the back of an envelope which I later lost, though I still remembered most of it. But that's rarely enough, and so it proved in this case.

So, back again. What if I sell part of the portfolio, let's say the equivalent of £50 000 (500 units times market value £100)? The £50 000 will go into the bank account earning 5% interest.

| **I sell 500 units of my portfolio at £100 releasing £50 000 to be put in the bank account earning 5% interest** | **£** |
|---|---|
| Fund value at the beginning | 950 000 |
| Cash value at the beginning | 50 000 |
| Total value at the beginning | 1 000 000 |
| MARKET CHANGE after 30 days | −3% |
| New fund value | 873 000 |
| New cash value | 100 416 |
| New total value | 973 416 |
| TOTAL VALUE CHANGE | −26 584 |
| PERCENT VALUE CHANGE | −2.66% |

Of course, if I reduce my exposure, which I do when I sell shares, I should incur smaller losses than if I didn't do anything. The example with a 7% fall should substantiate that.

| **I sell 500 units of my portfolio at £100 releasing £50 000 to be put in the bank account earning 5% interest** | **£** |
|---|---|
| Fund value at the beginning | 950 000 |
| Cash value at the beginning | 50 000 |
| Total value at the beginning | 1 000 000 |
| MARKET CHANGE after 30 days | −7% |
| New fund value | 837 000 |
| New cash value | 100 416 |
| New total value | 937 416 |
| TOTAL VALUE CHANGE | −62 584 |
| PERCENT VALUE CHANGE | −6.26% |

Yes, it did in percentage terms. Now, the next example is an interesting one. Instead of selling shares and putting the cash in the bank, I can sell some shares and buy others to reduce the sensitivity to market movements, i.e. the correlation to market changes – reduce the beta I suppose. So far, my portfolio has been 100% correlated to market movements – Market100. If I now reduce the correlation to 95%, how will that change the outcome in the two scenarios?

| **I sell some shares and buy others so that my exposure to market movements is reduced from a correlation of 100% to 95%** | **£** |
|---|---|
| Fund value at the beginning | 950 000 |
| Cash value at the beginning | 50 000 |
| Total value at the beginning | 1 000 000 |
| MARKET CHANGE after 30 days | −3% |
| New fund value | 922 999 |
| New cash value | 50 208 |
| New total value | 973 208 |
| TOTAL VALUE CHANGE | −26 793 |
| PERCENT VALUE CHANGE | −2.68% |

Seems to be in the ballpark of the other scenarios or strategies. Why bother? No, let's keep an open mind. This is an ongoing process – gain after gain after gain after gain will do it. That's how I'll be successful. (I suppose there'll be the odd loss as well, but as long as the gains are greater and more frequent, I'll live with that.) On to the 7% fall.

| **I sell some shares and buy others so that my exposure to market movements is reduced from a correlation of 100% to 95%** | **£** |
|---|---|
| Fund value at the beginning | 950 000 |
| Cash value at the beginning | 50 000 |
| Total value at the beginning | 1 000 000 |
| MARKET CHANGE after 30 days | −7% |
| New fund value | 886 998 |
| New cash value | 50 208 |
| New total value | 937 206 |
| TOTAL VALUE CHANGE | −62 794 |
| PERCENT VALUE CHANGE | −6.28% |

Yes, just confirmed the message. I dread this moment. I went for a walk, made unnecessary phone calls, had a cup of tea and you name it. I was anxious. My theory about derivatives being superior, would it hold in reality? Stop fussing, just get on with it.

I took another break, made a cup of tea and sat down to listen to some music. It was a 1980s compilation and my mind drifted back to wild university years. Then I fell asleep.

Woke up and returned to the dreaded calculations. Boring as hell, but I need to work through them. So onto the first calculation involving options.

| **I buy put options (at the money). Strike price 100. The put option costs 1.3861 (the premium I have to pay) at the beginning (45 days to expiry). I wish to hedge £50 000, so I buy 50 contracts of put options (each contract is 100 units) with strike price 100** | **£** |
|---|---|
| Fund value at the beginning | 950 000 |
| Premium paid for put options | 694 |
| Cash value at the beginning | 49 306 |
| Total value at the beginning | 1 000 000 |
| MARKET CHANGE after 30 days | −3% |
| New fund value | 921 500 |
| Put option value | 1 469 |
| New cash value | 49 511 |
| New total value | 972 480 |
| TOTAL VALUE CHANGE | −27 520 |
| PERCENT VALUE CHANGE | −2.75% |

That one didn't do much good, did it? Then again, it's a short period of time – only 30 days – and a very small part of the portfolio hedged. Let's see what the outcome of the 7% fall gives us before we really slag things off.

| **I buy put options (at the money). Strike price 100. The put option costs 1.3861 (the premium I have to pay) at the beginning (45 days to expiry). I wish to hedge £50 000, so I buy 50 contracts of put options (each contract is 100 units) with strike price 100** | **£** |
|---|---|
| Fund value at the beginning | 950 000 |
| Premium paid for put options | 694 |
| Cash value at the beginning | 49 306 |
| Total value at the beginning | 1 000 000 |
| MARKET CHANGE after 30 days | −7% |
| New fund value | 883 500 |
| Put option value | 3 398 |
| New cash value | 49 511 |
| New total value | 936 409 |
| TOTAL VALUE CHANGE | −63 591 |
| PERCENT VALUE CHANGE | −6.36% |

No massive improvement. I suppose I need to hedge a bigger part of the portfolio; it seems the more I hedge, the more I win (or the more I reduce the fall in portfolio value). If that's true, let's buy 500 options contracts, effectively hedging £500 000 of the portfolio value – half the total portfolio, oops.

| **I buy put options (at the money). Strike price 100. The put option costs 1.3861 (the premium I have to pay) at the beginning (45 days to expiry). I wish to hedge £500 000, so I buy 500 contracts of put options (each contract is 100 units) with strike price 100** | **£** |
|---|---|
| Fund value at the beginning | 950 000 |
| Premium paid for put options | 6 931 |
| Cash value at the beginning | 43 069 |
| Total value at the beginning | 1 000 000 |
| MARKET CHANGE after 30 days | −3% |
| New fund value | 921 500 |
| Put option value | 14 691 |
| New cash value | 43 248 |
| New total value | 979 439 |
| TOTAL VALUE CHANGE | −20 561 |
| PERCENT VALUE CHANGE | −2.06% |

That's more like it. Let's check the 7% example.

| **I buy put options (at the money). Strike price 100. The put option costs 1.3861 (the premium I have to pay) at the beginning (45 days to expiry). I wish to hedge £500 000, so I buy 500 contracts of put options (each contract is 100 units) with strike price 100** | **£** |
|---|---|
| Fund value at the beginning | 950 000 |
| Premium paid for put options | 6 931 |
| Cash value at the beginning | 43 069 |
| Total value at the beginning | 1 000 000 |
| MARKET CHANGE after 30 days | −7% |
| New fund value | 883 500 |
| Put option value | 33 980 |
| New cash value | 43 248 |
| New total value | 960 728 |
| TOTAL VALUE CHANGE | −39 272 |
| PERCENT VALUE CHANGE | −3.93% |

Suppose I buy put options out of the money, instead of at the money. Well, if the market price is 100 and I buy put options with strike price 100, they're said to be at the money. If instead I buy options with a strike price of 95, I buy options out of the money. Since at the money put options give me the right to sell at a strike price in line with the underlying market price, they are more 'expensive' than out of the money options. Out of the money options will require a further fall to 'get going'.

| **I buy put options (out of the money). Strike price 95. The put option costs 0.1625 (the premium I have to pay) at the beginning (45 days to expiry). I wish to hedge £500 000, so I buy 500 contracts of put options (each contract is 100 units) with strike price 100** | **£** |
|---|---|
| Fund value at the beginning | 950 000 |
| Premium paid for put options | 813 |
| Cash value at the beginning | 49 187 |
| Total value at the beginning | 1 000 000 |
| MARKET CHANGE after 30 days | −3% |
| New fund value | 921 500 |
| Put option value | 1 086 |
| New cash value | 49 392 |
| New total value | 971 978 |
| TOTAL VALUE CHANGE | −28 022 |
| PERCENT VALUE CHANGE | −2.80% |

Well, that didn't seem to be such a good idea. Let's look at the example when prices fall by 7%.

| **I buy put options (out of the money). Strike price 95. The put option costs 0.1625 (the premium I have to pay) at the beginning (45 days to expiry). I wish to hedge £500 000, so I buy 500 contracts of put options (each contract is 100 units) with strike price 100** | **£** |
|---|---|
| Fund value at the beginning | 950 000 |
| Premium paid for put options | 813 |
| Cash value at the beginning | 49 187 |
| Total value at the beginning | 1 000 000 |
| MARKET CHANGE after 30 days | −7% |
| New fund value | 883 500 |
| Put option value | 10 422 |
| New cash value | 49 392 |
| New total value | 943 314 |
| TOTAL VALUE CHANGE | −56 686 |
| PERCENT VALUE CHANGE | −5.67% |

Not as good as the at the money puts. I need to check the percentage change for the in the money options as opposed to the out of the money options in the two scenarios, −3% and −7%.

| **Put option** | **Initial premium** | **New value** | | **Change** | |
|---|---|---|---|---|---|
| | | **3% fall** | **7% fall** | **3% fall** | **7% fall** |
| At the money (100/100) | 1.3861 | 2.9382 | 6.7960 | **212%** | 490% |
| Out of the money (95/100) | 0.1625 | 0.2173 | 2.0845 | 134% | **1283%** |

All in all, the results aren't too bad. It seems that the leverage really picks up once options move from out of the money to at the money or in the money (which is when the strike price is higher than the underlying price for the put option). In pound terms, the at the money options give the best return, but bearing in mind that I could have bought roughly 8.5 times as many put options out of the money as at the money, that would probably swing things around. Let's check.

| Put option | Initial premium (£) | New value (£) | | Change | |
|---|---|---|---|---|---|
| | | 3% fall | 7% fall | 3% fall | 7% fall |
| At the money (100/100) 500 contracts | 6931 | **14 691** | 33 980 | **212%** | 490% |
| Out of the money (95/100) 4260 contracts | 6922 | 9 257 | **88 780** | 134% | **1 283%** |

By paying the same amount in premium, at the money options are more effective when the change in the market value is small, that is when the out of the money options never get in the money; whereas if a substantial decline is expected, out of the money options are more powerful. I should also bear in mind that even with the same exposure, 500 contracts, out of the money options are more powerful for significant market moves, i.e. where they move into the money. The added benefit will have to be that if I'm wrong buying only 500 contracts, the 'out of the money strategy' will cost me less. I'll have to come back to the evaluation of all strategies in a while. Tea break!

Now, as they stand, the options strategies provide a hedge for an unlimited fall in share prices, which may be unlikely. So, for a smaller decline, the premium I am paying may be rather high. A more realistic scenario may be to hedge for a fall in share prices by let's say 5%. Conceptually, this involves two separate options contracts at different strike prices. Step one would be as previously to buy a put option. Step two would be to write a put option at a lower strike price. The benefit of this strategy is that the premium I receive for the short put option will offset part of the premium I have to pay for the long put option at a higher strike price. Using the same starting point as for the earlier examples, the current market price is 100. I buy a put option at the strike price 100 (at the money) and write a put option at the strike price 95. In the earlier example, the premium paid was 1.3861 and I would receive 0.1625 for a short out of the money option at strike price 95. The net premium is 1.2236 or nearly a 12% reduction in premium outlay.

If the market falls by 3%, this strategy will pay 96% of just buying the put at strike 100. With a greater fall in the market – down to 93 or by 7% – this strategy only pays 64%, compared with the outright long put option. However, if the market goes the other way – it rises by 3% – then the loss will be only 87%, compared with just the long put option.

Now 3% is a significant change, but I believe this is telling me that if the market falls within my band, 5%, I receive close to what I would receive in the outright strategy; whereas if the fall is greater, 7%, i.e. 2 percentage points outside my band, the written option starts to cost me money. Then, if I was wrong altogether, and the market goes up instead of down, the combined strategy actually saves me around 12%.

| **I buy put options at strike 100 and write at strike 95. 500 contracts in both cases** | **£** |
|---|---|
| Fund value at the beginning | 950 000 |
| Net premium paid | 6 118 |
| Cash value at the beginning | 43 882 |
| Total value at the beginning | 1 000 000 |
| MARKET CHANGE after 30 days | −3% |
| New fund value | 921 500 |
| Net put option value | 13 604 |
| New cash value | 44 065 |
| New total value | 979 169 |
| TOTAL VALUE CHANGE | −20 831 |
| PERCENT VALUE CHANGE | −2.08% |

| **I buy put options at strike 100 and write at strike 95. 500 contracts in both cases** | **£** |
|---|---|
| Fund value at the beginning | 950 000 |
| Net premium paid | 6 118 |
| Cash value at the beginning | 43 882 |
| Total value at the beginning | 1 000 000 |
| MARKET CHANGE after 30 days | −7% |
| New fund value | 883 500 |
| Net put option value | 23 558 |
| New cash value | 44 065 |
| New total value | 951 123 |
| TOTAL VALUE CHANGE | −48 877 |
| PERCENT VALUE CHANGE | −4.89% |

This is the final evaluation chart.

| **Strategy** | **Market declines by 3%** | **Market declines by 7%** | **Market goes up by 3%** |
|---|---|---|---|
| Do nothing | −2.83 | −6.63 | **2.87** |
| Sell 500 units | −2.66 | −6.26 | 2.74 |
| Rebalance | −2.68 | −6.28 | 2.73 |
| Put options buy 50 contracts | −2.75 | −6.36 | 2.80 |
| Put options buy 500 contracts ATM | **−2.06** | **−3.93** | 2.17 |
| Put options buy 500 contracts out of the money | −2.80 | −5.67 | 2.79 |
| Put option strategy buy 500 ATM, write 500 out of the money | −2.08 | −4.89 | 2.26 |

ATM = at the money

It looks like the options strategies are quite useful as they don't offset too much of the value growth if the market goes up, but they could shave off a few percentage points of the decline in value when the market falls.

An alternative to buying put options to gain from falling markets is to write call options. If the market goes down, the call options will be useless to the buyer and the writer can pocket the premium. However, the upside is limited to the premium and if the market goes up instead, the downside – potential loss – is unlimited.

## 5 May 2000

As with falling markets, there are different strategies that can be used when markets are expected to rise. Here are the four strategies I'll explore:

– I don't do anything.
– I invest the cash part of the portfolio bringing the portfolio up to 100%.
– I rebalance the portfolio to increase 'correlation' or sensitivity to market changes to represent a 100% portfolio holding.
– I buy call options on market index (benchmark).

The examples are based on the same conditions as I used when the market was falling, i.e. total funds of £1 000 000, of which 95% is invested in Market100 constituents, replicating the index to 100%. The current value of Market100 is 100. So £950 000 is invested in shares (I have 9500 units of Market100) and £50 000 is held in cash. The interest rate for cash is 5% annually. The investment period is 30 days. I use a volatility of 12% as in the earlier calculations.

Let's start with the do-nothing strategy.

| **I don't do anything** | **£** |
|---|---|
| Fund value at the beginning | 950 000 |
| Cash value at the beginning | 50 000 |
| Total value at the beginning | 1 000 000 |
| MARKET CHANGE after 30 days | +3% |
| New fund value | 978 500 |
| New cash value | 50 208 |
| New total value | 1 028 708 |
| TOTAL VALUE CHANGE | 28 708 |
| PERCENT VALUE CHANGE | +2.87% |

That seems reasonable, 2.87%; I hold £50K in cash. With a 7% market rise, the change in value should be just below 7% if my reasoning is correct. Let's have a look.

| **I don't do anything** | **£** |
|---|---|
| Fund value at the beginning | 950 000 |
| Cash value at the beginning | 50 000 |
| Total value at the beginning | 1 000 000 |
| MARKET CHANGE after 30 days | +7% |
| New fund value | 1 016 500 |
| New cash value | 50 208 |
| New total value | 1 066 708 |
| TOTAL VALUE CHANGE | +66 708 |
| PERCENT VALUE CHANGE | +6.67% |

Yes, + 6.67%, as I expected. But what if I gear up and invest everything in my fund? I invest my £50 000 cash in my fund.

It was a gorgeous day and I needed a break. My good side suggested I should go for a run. I put on my trainers but then I went down to the village pub. I had a few pints of lager while playing or rather practising my self-invented game of dart golf. The rules are easy. You have three darts and start with number 1 through to 20. All three darts are first aimed at number 1. A score of 2 per number is par for that number. A treble obviously takes you one below par, and so on. The best I managed for a full round of 1–20 was 8 over par, about halfway through the session. After the third pint I decided to finish and go for a walk instead. By then my arm was feeling numb anyway.

Back at the desk for more calculations. Where were we? Yes, gear up by investing it all in shares.

| **I invest the £50 000 cash in Market100 shares** | **£** |
|---|---|
| Fund value at the beginning | 1 000 000 |
| Cash value at the beginning | 0 |
| Total value at the beginning | 1 000 000 |
| MARKET CHANGE after 30 days | +3% |
| New fund value | 1 030 000 |
| New cash value | 0 |
| New total value | 1 030 000 |
| TOTAL VALUE CHANGE | +30 000 |
| PERCENT VALUE CHANGE | +3.00% |

Spot on! Of course, now my portfolio moves completely in line with the market. The same should apply for the 7% scenario as well.

| **I invest the £50 000 cash in Market100 shares** | **£** |
|---|---|
| Fund value at the beginning | 1 000 000 |
| Cash value at the beginning | 0 |
| Total value at the beginning | 1 000 000 |
| MARKET CHANGE after 30 days | +7% |
| New fund value | 1 070 000 |
| New cash value | 70 000 |
| New total value | 1 070 000 |
| TOTAL VALUE CHANGE | +70 000 |
| PERCENT VALUE CHANGE | +7.00% |

Obviously, a value change of 7%.

| **I rebalance the portfolio so that the correlation increases from 100% to 105%** | **£** |
|---|---|
| Fund value at the beginning | 950 000 |
| Cash value at the beginning | 50 000 |
| Total value at the beginning | 1 000 000 |
| MARKET CHANGE after 30 days | +3% |
| New fund value | 979 925 |
| New cash value | 50 208 |
| New total value | 1 030 133 |
| TOTAL VALUE CHANGE | +30 133 |
| PERCENT VALUE CHANGE | +3.03% |

| **I rebalance the portfolio so that the correlation increases from 100% to 105%** | **£** |
|---|---|
| Fund value at the beginning | 950 000 |
| Cash value at the beginning | 50 000 |
| Total value at the beginning | 1 000 000 |
| MARKET CHANGE after 30 days | +7% |
| New fund value | 1 019 825 |
| New cash value | 50 208 |
| New total value | 1 070 033 |
| TOTAL VALUE CHANGE | +70 033 |
| PERCENT VALUE CHANGE | +7.00% |

The rebalancing gives pretty much the same result as taking the cash pot and investing it in Market100 shares, similar to the example with the put options.

| **I buy call options (at the money). Strike price 100. The call options cost 2.0006 (the premium I have to pay) at the beginning (45 days to expiry). I wish to increase exposure by £50 000, so I buy 50 contracts of call options (each contract is 100 units) with strike price 100** | **£** |
|---|---|
| Fund value at the beginning | 950 000 |
| Premium paid for call options | 1 001 |
| Cash value at the beginning | 48 999 |
| Total value at the beginning | 1 000 000 |
| MARKET CHANGE after 30 days | +3% |
| New fund value | 978 500 |
| Call option value | 1 659 |
| New cash value | 49 203 |
| New total value | 1 029 362 |
| TOTAL VALUE CHANGE | +£29 362 |
| PERCENT VALUE CHANGE | +2.94% |

Compared to doing nothing, the result with some call options is a bit better, 2.94% instead of 2.87%.

| **I buy call options (at the money). Strike price 100. The call options cost 2.0006 (the premium I have to pay) at the beginning (45 days to expiry). I wish to increase exposure by £50 000, so I buy 50 contracts of call options (each contract is 100 units) with strike price 100** | **£** |
|---|---|
| Fund value at the beginning | 950 000 |
| Premium paid for call options | 1 001 |
| Cash value at the beginning | 48 999 |
| Total value at the beginning | 1 000 000 |
| MARKET CHANGE after 30 days | +7% |
| New fund value | 1 016 500 |
| Call option value | 3 603 |
| New cash value | 49 203 |
| New total value | 1 069 306 |
| TOTAL VALUE CHANGE | +69 306 |
| PERCENT VALUE CHANGE | +6.93% |

The call options are adding even more value when the market change is more significant, which is as expected.

What if I bought futures instead? Well, the upside should be in line with the long call options without having to pay the premium. On the other hand, if the market moves south, the loss potential won't be limited to the premium. In all, a bit too risky for my purposes.

| **I buy call options (at the money). Strike price 100. The call options cost 2.0006 (the premium I have to pay) at the beginning (45 days to expiry). I wish to increase exposure by £500 000, so I buy 500 contracts of call options (each contract is 100 units) with strike price 100** | **£** |
|---|---|
| Fund value at the beginning | 950 000 |
| Premium paid for call options | 10 003 |
| Cash value at the beginning | 39 997 |
| Total value at the beginning | 1 000 000 |
| MARKET CHANGE after 30 days | +3% |
| New fund value | 978 500 |
| Call option value | 16 589 |
| New cash value | 40 164 |
| New total value | 1 035 253 |
| TOTAL VALUE CHANGE | +35 253 |
| PERCENT VALUE CHANGE | +3.52% |

With an increased call option position we're getting better results. Now the portfolio outperforms the market for the first time.

| **I buy call options (at the money). Strike price 100. The call options cost 2.0006 (the premium I have to pay) at the beginning (45 days to expiry). I wish to increase exposure by £500 000 so I buy 500 contracts of call options (each contract is 100 units) with strike price 100** | **£** |
|---|---|
| Fund value at the beginning | 950 000 |
| Premium paid for call options | 10 003 |
| Cash value at the beginning | 39 997 |
| Total value at the beginning | 1 000 000 |
| MARKET CHANGE after 30 days | +7% |
| New fund value | 1 016 500 |
| Call option value | 36 034 |
| New cash value | 40 164 |
| New total value | 1 092 698 |
| TOTAL VALUE CHANGE | +92 698 |
| PERCENT VALUE CHANGE | +9.27% |

Again, more significant when the market movement is greater. Here the value is 2.27 percentage points greater than the gain in the market, which is 7%.

| **I buy call options (out of the money). Strike price 105. The call options cost 0.3508 (the premium I have to pay) at the beginning (45 days to expiry). I wish to increase exposure by £500 000, so I buy 500 contracts of call options (each contract is 100 units) with strike price 100** | **£** |
|---|---|
| Fund value at the beginning | 950 000 |
| Premium paid for call options | 1 754 |
| Cash value at the beginning | 48 246 |
| Total value at the beginning | 1 000 000 |
| MARKET CHANGE after 30 days | +3% |
| New fund value | 978 500 |
| Call option value | 1 787 |
| New cash value | 48 447 |
| New total value | 1 028 734 |
| TOTAL VALUE CHANGE | +28 734 |
| PERCENT VALUE CHANGE | +2.87% |

As expected.

Before wrapping up the maths session, I need another break. Edward and James have come home from school, so I'll play some football in the garden with them.

They're too good. I got soundly beaten and had another beer as consolation. I need to improve my level of fitness. I'll think about that another time. Back to the calcs!

| **I buy call options (out of the money). Strike price 105. The call options cost 0.3508 (the premium I have to pay) at the beginning (45 days to expiry). I wish to increase exposure by £500 000, so I buy 500 contracts of call options (each contract is 100 units) with strike price 100** | **£** |
|---|---|
| Fund value at the beginning | 950 000 |
| Premium paid for call options | 1 754 |
| Cash value at the beginning | 48 246 |
| Total value at the beginning | 1 000 000 |
| MARKET CHANGE after 30 days | +7% |
| New fund value | 1 016 500 |
| Call option value | 12 469 |
| New cash value | 48 447 |
| New total value | 1 077 416 |
| TOTAL VALUE CHANGE | +77 416 |
| PERCENT VALUE CHANGE | +7.74% |

Managed to beat the market, but not the at the money strategy.

| **Call option** | **Initial premium** | **New value** | | **Change** | |
|---|---|---|---|---|---|
| | | **3% rise** | **7% rise** | **3% rise** | **7% rise** |
| At the money (100/100) | 2.0006 | 3.3177 | 7.2068 | **166%** | 360% |
| Out of the money (105/100) | 0.3508 | 0.3575 | 2.4938 | 102% | **711%** |

| Call option | Initial premium (£) | New value (£) | | Change | |
|---|---|---|---|---|---|
| | | 3% rise | 7% rise | 3% rise | 7% rise |
| At the money (100/100) 500 contracts | 10 003 | **16 589** | 36 034 | **166%** | 360% |
| Out of the money (105/100) 2852 contracts | 10 003 | 10 194 | **71 110** | 102% | **711%** |

At the money calls are more effective than out of the money calls for smaller market movements, whereas the latter are rather more powerful with greater market movements, particularly if the same premium is spent on the out of the money calls as the at the money calls. Here's the final evaluation chart of my call option calculations.

| Strategy | Market rises by 3% | Market rises by 7% | Market declines by 3% |
|---|---|---|---|
| Do nothing | 2.87 | 6.67 | **−2.83** |
| Buy 500 units | 3.00 | 7.00 | −3.00 |
| Rebalance | 3.03 | 7.00 | −2.97 |
| Call options buy 50 contracts | 2.94 | 6.93 | −2.92 |
| Call options buy 500 contracts ATM | **3.52** | **9.27** | −3.76 |
| Call options buy 500 contracts out of the money | 2.87 | 7.74 | −3.01 |

ATM = at the money

The options strategies are useful to gain exposure, especially when it may take time to build a position or when single companies are sought after. They offer far better value than rebalancing, thanks to the leverage, but principally when the position is significant – 500 contracts rather than 50 contracts and large movements rather than small movements. When you're right, i.e. you buy puts when the market is going down or, as in this case, you buy calls when the market is going up, at the money options offer the best value. However, if you're wrong and the market goes the other way, I'm sad to say, the do-nothing strategy offers the best value out of the alternatives I've checked so far.

## 9 May 2000

When it comes to stable and dull markets, options are outstanding in creating value. If I believe the market is not going to move significantly over the next month, I can choose a strategy that will enhance my portfolio performance by writing both call options and put options at the same strike price (at the money) and of the same expiry month.

Here the starting point for the example should be the same.

| Activity | Premium received | Value @ market price 100 after 30 days | Value @ market price 97 after 30 days | Value @ market price 103 after 30 days |
|---|---|---|---|---|
| Sell put option @ strike 100 | 1.3861 | 0.8704 | 2.9382 | 0.1124 |
| Sell call option @ strike 100 | 2.0006 | 1.0756 | 0.1435 | 3.3177 |
| Total value | 3.3867 | 1.946 | 3.0817 | 3.4301 (losing money) |

The net gain is the difference between what I receive (column 1) and the market value (any one of columns 2 to 4).

My break-even range is 96.65–102.90. However, when the market gets quieter, volatility should drop, which will probably extend my break-even range a bit. If the volatility dropped from 12% to 7%, my lower break-even level would be 96.45, a bit better.

I think I'm onto something in terms of strategies. It's an area I need to look into a bit more.

# CHAPTER THREE

## 25 May 2000

The whole idea behind options strategies as opposed to outright options is to balance the premium payment. Through a strategy I can adjust the risk profile so it still fits with the overall scenario, but it eliminates or at least significantly reduces the premium outlay. There are certain strategies for different markets – bullish (going up), bearish (going down) and undecided (like me). For each of these markets I'll examine what to do when I expect volatility to go up, go down or when I don't know where it's going.

Let's start with the bullish market – I love bullish markets. Don't know why, I just do.

**Ratio call back spread (when volatility is expected to go up) – an alternative to long call**

Sell a call and buy two higher strike calls of the same expiry month

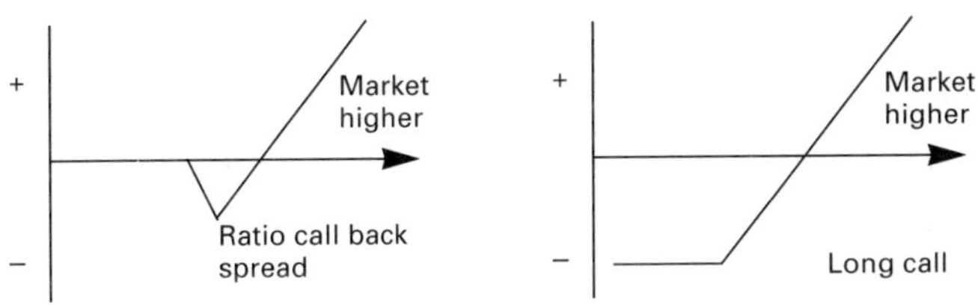

**Ratio put spread (when volatility is expected to go down) – alternative to short put**

Buy a put and sell two lower strike puts of the same delivery month

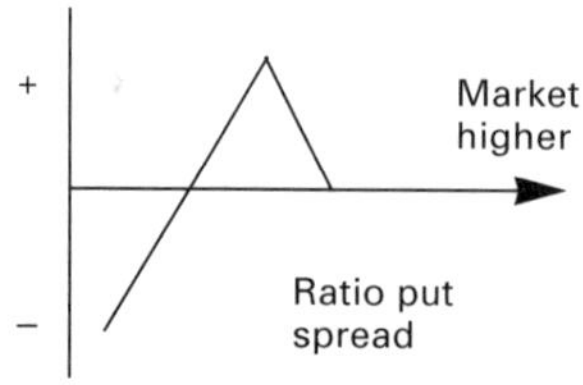


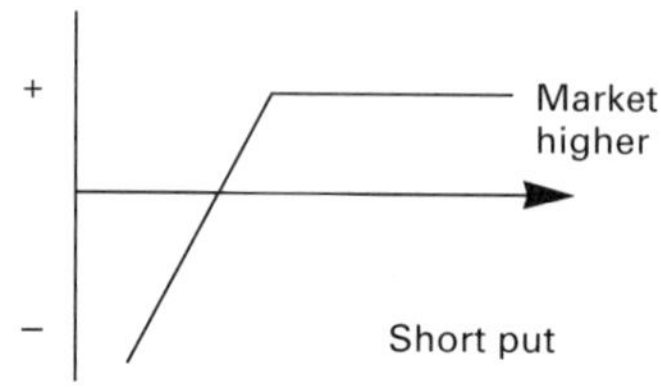


**Bull spread (when volatility is undecided) – alternative to long futures contract**

Buy a call and sell a call at a higher strike, or
Buy a put and sell a put at a higher strike of the same delivery month

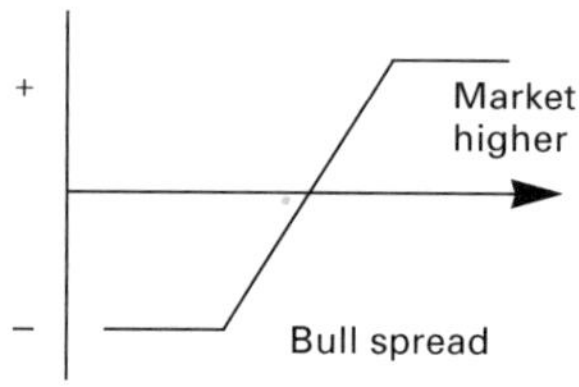


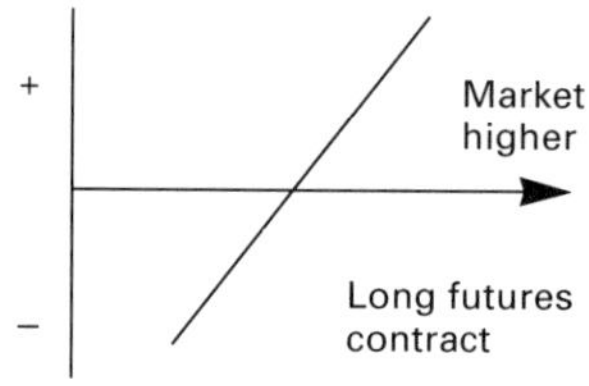


Next I've found some useful strategies for bearish markets.

**Ratio put back spread (when volatility is expected to go up) – an alternative to long put**

Sell a put and buy two lower strike puts of the same expiry month

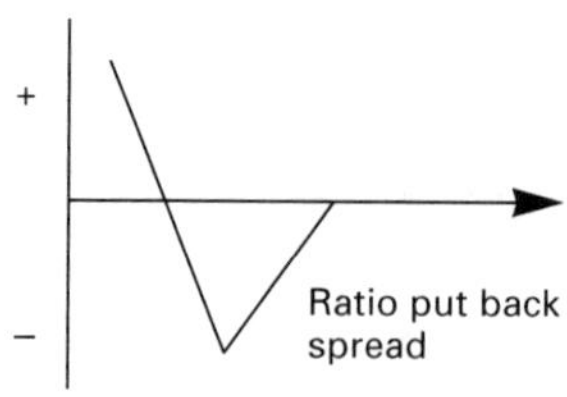


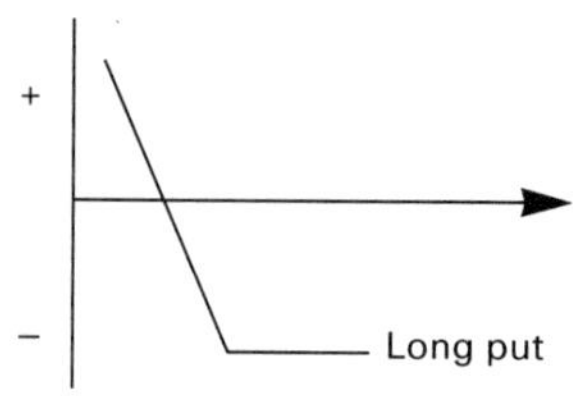

**Ratio call spread (when volatility is expected to go down) – alternative to short call**

Buy a call and sell two higher strike calls of the same delivery month

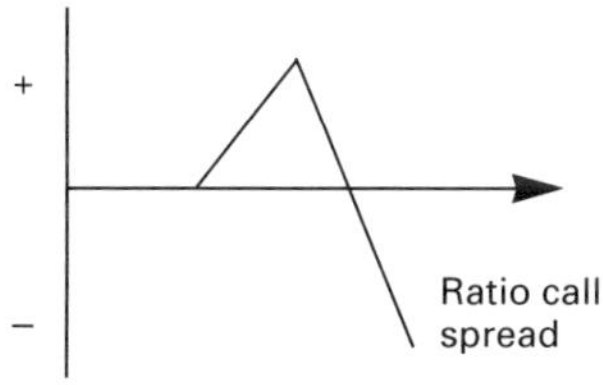


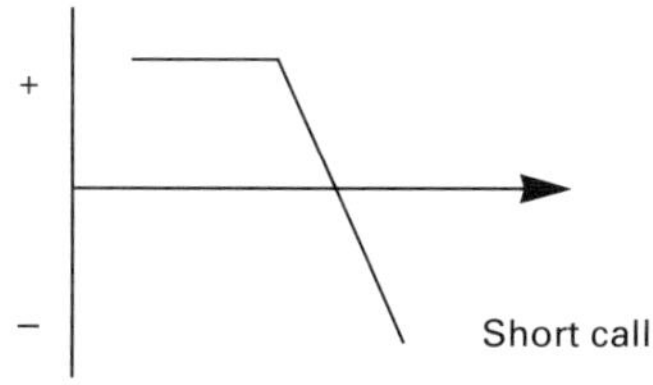


**Bear spread (when volatility is undecided) – alternative to short futures contract**

Buy a put and sell a put at a lower strike, or
Buy a call and sell a call at a lower strike of the same delivery month

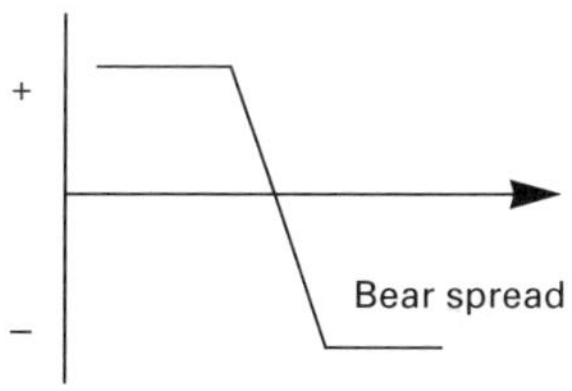


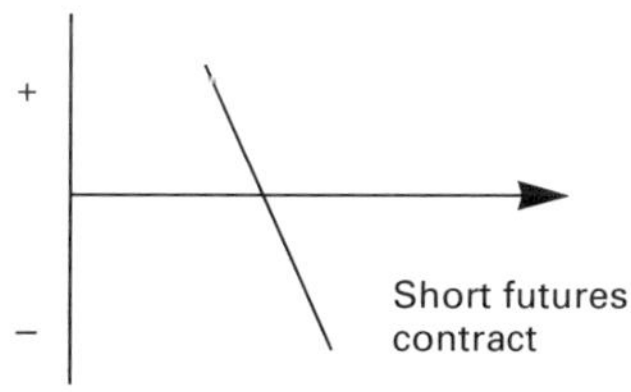


When it comes to undecided markets, it could either be that the market is going to calm down to lower volatility, or that pressure is building up for a breakout to higher volatility, but the direction is unclear. I've found a few very useful strategies.

**Long straddle (when volatility is expected to go up)**

Buy call and buy put at the same strike and of the same expiry month

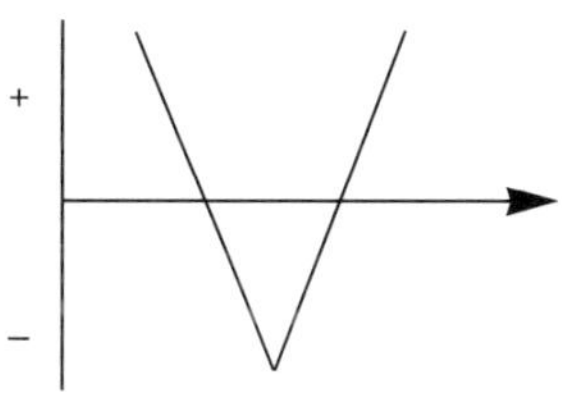

**Long strangle (when volatility is expected to go up)**

Buy higher strike call and buy lower strike put of the same delivery month

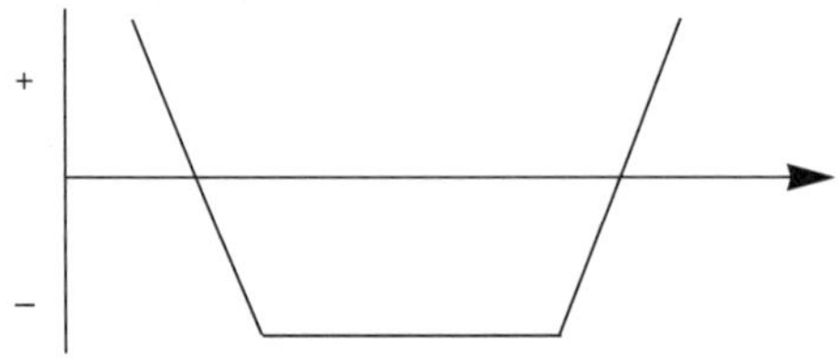

**Short straddle (when volatility is expected to go down)**

Sell call and sell put at the same strike and of the same delivery month

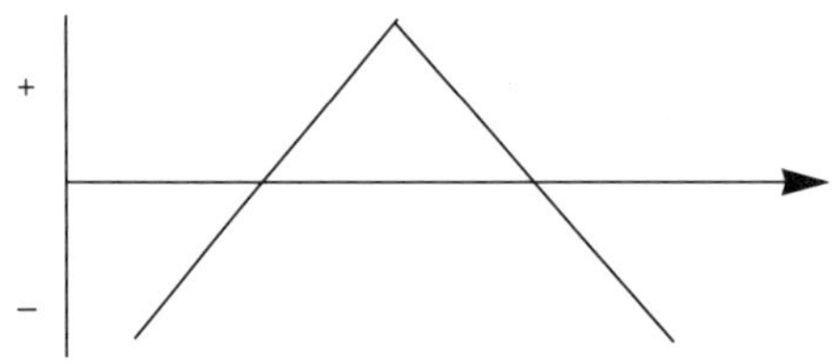

**Short strangle (when volatility is expected to go down)**

Sell higher strike call and sell lower strike put of the same delivery month

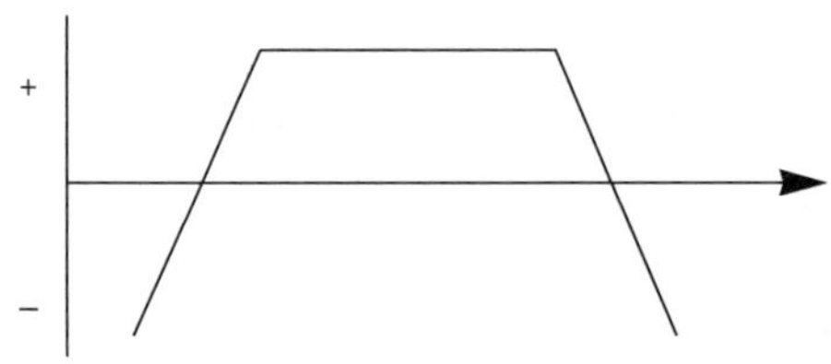

All dandy, but what if both market and volatility are undecided? The books didn't provide any clear guidance on this, and in all fairness, with all that uncertainty it's probably best to watch the market. I would not be surprised if premiums were on the high side to accommodate all the uncertainty. Another reason to stay away.

# CHAPTER FOUR

## 6 June 2000

I'm starting to feel things are progressing. I've decided to spend the next week or so focusing on the word 'risk'. What is risk? How do you define risk? And more importantly, how do you measure and manage risk? Semantically, isn't 'risk' the opposite of 'chance', like in 'there's a good chance I'll meet him there'. I suppose you could say 'there's a risk I won't see him there', which probably would be the reflection of a pessimist, whereas the first sentence would be that of an optimist. Someone once told me, 'Don't invest money you can't afford to be without' and I suppose that is very much what it's all about. The obvious risk-free investment is to keep your money in an instant savings account. Your investment is safe and you'll earn some interest, even if there is some uncertainty over the eventual amount.

I went to look in one of my old school books and there the standard risk-free asset was a Treasury bill. T-bills are discount papers, that is you buy them at a discount, e.g. 95.50 and they will mature at a price of 100 sometime later. There is a new element introduced with the T-bill and that is time. You are only certain to get back the money you invested plus the interest you were 'promised' when you bought the T-bill if you hold it to maturity. The book went on to discuss investments over longer periods, for example five years. You can't find T-bills with that maturity, since they normally don't go beyond 12 months. If you still want to invest in T-bills, the risk you face is the reinvestment risk. You need to reinvest your original investment plus accrued interest four times, so even if you can meet your return target in year one, you are not certain to do it over and over again.

A better investment for this purpose would be a bond. Now, the book went on, there are two basic types of bond – coupon bonds and zero-coupon bonds. Coupon bonds carry annual (or semi-annual) interest in the form of a coupon, that is interest paid to you, whereas the zero-coupon bond doesn't pay any interest during its life, but rather like the T-bill, the price is discounted and it matures at a price of 100. The coupon bond eliminates the hassle of reinvesting the principal amount over and over, but it doesn't address the need to reinvest the coupon payments. Hence there is still some uncertainty or risk if you so wish. Only the zero-coupon bond held to maturity guarantees that the return is actually what you opted for when you bought the bond.

It is important to have a clear picture of the time horizon. Although I believe my fund, or indeed funds, will keep going for quite a while, I must understand the needs of my clients. People close to retirement should not be exposed to high-risk or long-term investments, whereas younger people like most of my friends and contacts from the market would be well suited by higher risk. I suppose the idea with an investment horizon works perfectly with bonds and other instruments with a fixed maturity, but how about equities? They are perpetual or at least live until the company in question is bought by another company or goes belly up. There's no given maturity. I'd better check this with Tony since he's in risk management. I phoned him and we agreed to meet later tonight at his place.

'Hello, Thomas, do come in!' said Helen, Tony's wife. 'How are you and the family? I haven't seen Amanda for ages. Is she okay?'

'Yes, thank you, we're all just fine.'

Then Tony saved me by shouting, 'Thomas, come on in. I'm in the kitchen.' We grabbed a beer each and sat down in the adjoining conservatory. 'So Thomas, you're on to the concept of risk now. How can I help you, mate?'

'Well, I have to cover my bases. I've got to refresh my understanding of the theory behind risk and in particular derivatives. It's one thing to work these things in the professional market, where everyone is at the same level of understanding. I've got to sell my ideas to people who don't necessarily have a good understanding of these things. And to be absolutely honest, that's not a requirement as long as they have some dough to spare. But for me, this is key. I need to understand this to be able to explain it in an easily understandable fashion. I was going through the old school books earlier today and came across the idea of risk-free investments and all that. In that context, a bond, which has longer maturity is more risky than a T-bill. An immediate change in interest rates by 1% results in approximately a 1% decline in the price of a one-year T-bill and a decline of just over 4% in the price of a five-year par bond. The question that struck me earlier today was, How can you explain or compare equities with bonds on this basis?'

'My dear Thomas, you can't compare interest rate investments with equities in that way. The price of equities doesn't have such a clear relationship with another factor. The way to compare bonds and equities is to look at historical data. Rather, you could look at the price volatility in different assets and find that the higher the volatility, the riskier the investment. Stock markets are generally more volatile and it's not surprising to see changes between 2% and 4% from one day to another, whereas a similar change in the price of a five-year bond would require five-year interest rates to change by 0.5% to 1%. It's not impossible and I'm not saying it's never happened, but it's an extreme change in sentiment required to push the market by that much, as you well know.'

We carried on discussing risks for a while, but soon went on to more mundane things such as Tony's wild idea to take up five-a-side football. I told him he was crazy, but he seemed to really enjoy it and said he felt much fitter since he started playing a few weeks ago.

## 7 June 2000

I got up early to have some time on my own before the rest of the family woke up. By early I mean 5.30am. Normally the boys wake up at 7.30 except at weekends, when they wake up between 6.30 and 7.00. I think it's because they're allowed to stay up a bit longer on Fridays and Saturdays. But it doesn't seem to make sense – they go to bed later and wake up earlier. Nevertheless, I thought about my discussion with Tony last night and began to work on the relationship between stock markets and interest rates: when interest rates go up, stock markets go down. This is believed to be a consequence of higher interest rates attracting capital from the stock market, because bonds and other interest rate products give you a higher return at a lower risk. However, when interest rates are low, stock markets attract capital, so falling interest rates encourage stock markets to go up. But surely companies are sensitive to changes in interest rates and, more importantly, the level of interest rates. Bank shares seem to react to changes in interest rates; for example, if interest rates go down, banks are believed to make money on their bond portfolios, hence bank shares go up.

To further clarify this relationship, I had to consult my old school book on macroeconomics, which clearly spelled it out for me. High interest rates lead to a lower willingness to invest in companies and businesses, because of the attractiveness to invest in bonds and short-term interest rate products. This is called 'crowding out'. A long period of high interest rates will result in lower and lower investments, hence reduced chances to develop new products and services that can increase the revenue and eventually the value of a company; this will be expressed in the price of that company's shares.

I put the kettle on and sat down to read the morning paper. One of the main stories was the mounting concern among industrial and manufacturing leaders that the high pound is beginning to hurt British industry and that, in an official survey, a majority of the UK business leaders predicted a rapid decline in production and sales. All attention was now directed towards the Bank of England in a desperate attempt to persuade it to lower interest rates. I doubt their lobbying will be successful, but the article does seem to show that the relationship between interest rates and share prices actually holds in reality. However, I'm not entirely convinced a strong pound is all bad. Need to check that with Mick Brown, chief economist at GlobalBank. That's a good bit of networking. I'll probably ask him out for lunch.

## 8 June 2000

Woke up early again. Tonight Ben is coming round for dinner. Sort something out with Amanda. Need to think through what I want to discuss with Ben workwise. I don't want to spoil the whole evening, but I'm sure he won't mind telling me some stories and truths about risk. I need to explore credit risk, currency risk, systematic and non-systematic risk, and asymmetric risk.

It was a beautiful sunny morning, so I decided to go for a run. First I had to negotiate a very long and steep hill that changed into a flat part to end in a long downhill stretch back to the house. About halfway along the flat I saw something in the road; it looked like a small animal. At first it didn't seem injured, but when I got closer I realised it was a squirrel whose head had been crushed by a car. Apart from that, it wasn't harmed at all. So much for timing, I thought.

I went back to consult the old textbook for some more definitions and clarifications on the different types of risk. Credit risk, it said, is associated with the risk that a company defaults, which means it cannot repay outstanding debt. In the bond and short-term interest rate market, this risk is often measured by credit rating. Bonds and commercial papers issued by companies more likely to default have a lower rating than companies less likely to default, expressing a higher risk and leading to lower prices on these assets. Company debt is often compared with the Treasury markets – T-bills and gilts – expressed as the yield of the Treasury instrument plus a margin. What it tells us is that companies will have to pay a higher cost than the government for the money they borrow. Rating agencies will in most markets provide a qualitative rating of companies and the higher the rating, the lower the margin over Treasury debt.

Shares are not rated in this way. Some companies may have commercial paper programmes or other debt outstanding, and these too may have been rated; nevertheless, shares are the most risky of all investments and therefore they are most closely related to the performance of the company. I suppose history, in some sense, is not the best of tools to measure the risk of shares, because all companies listed to date have a more or less healthy life behind them. Some companies have a longer history than others, but the age of a company is not an accurate measure of its future stability and success. Rather the quality of a company should be reflected in the share price. I'll discuss this with Ben. Maybe he has some good ideas on how to address credit or default risk when investing in shares.

While I was searching the textbooks for a definition of currency risk, I came across the beast of beasts, or 'risk risk'. This was too much. In my entire career I have never come across anything like risk risk before. Although my curiosity was killing me, I took a break. I went downstairs and put the kettle on. Time for a nice cup of tea.

I returned to the books and went to the definition of risk risk. Risk risk was quite simply defined as not knowing what is the risk of a security or investment. I suppose you could say it's the epitome of risk, the whole point of asking all these questions. By finding the answers I would avoid, eliminate or at least significantly reduce my risk risk. Not knowing what I was doing or was going to do in my business was exactly what I was trying to avoid by this risk exercise. Learning to understand different types of risk was crucial. It was not necessary to remember all the definitions, which seemed to change over time.

Although Amanda did most of the cooking, I took an interest

when I had the time. We decided to do asparagus with salmon roe and crème fraiche for starters, followed by salmon steaks wrapped in Parma ham, with rice and spinach timbales and a fresh salad. For dessert a light passion fruit and Campari sorbet followed by cheese and biscuits. Normally, Amanda and I would have cheese before the dessert – I suppose it's something we've picked up on our many holidays to France – but with Ben coming I was hoping to do the shop-talking bit before having coffee, and to finish off with cheese offered the most flexibility.

Ben was on time as usual. He was known always to be on time, a man of routine and strong habits. Travelling upset his routine and that's probably why he tried to limit his business trips, although not very successfully, as he was so sought after. Privately, he would spend as much time as possible at his lakeside cottage in Vermont; fishing was one of his great pastimes. It always surprised me that Ben never got married, because he was such a jovial and easy-going character, but maybe the routines and habits and his overpowering control of any situation made it difficult for anyone to get really close in the sense of sharing his life.

Amanda had met Ben on a few occasions before and thoroughly enjoyed his company. We had a lovely dinner and once the cheese and biscuits were on the table I took my opportunity. 'Ben, I've kept a few bottles of port for special occasions and I feel this is one. How about the two of us withdrawing to the living room for a while and if you don't mind, I'll ask your advice on a couple of things.'

'Sure,' he replied, 'But what about Amanda? She wouldn't approve of that, would she?'

'As a matter of fact she would. I've promised to do all the business talking over the cheese and biscuits. We'll join her for coffee later on.'

I opened a bottle of 1974 Fonseca's and poured three glasses. I brought one over to Amanda and went back to start my discussion with Ben.

'Ben, I've been refreshing my knowledge of risk and I'd like to make sure I understand the relevant aspects. I need to avoid risk risk, which is the risk of not knowing what risks I will encounter in my new business. I've done the obvious by consulting my old textbooks, but these things seem to change and develop over time. I've covered some of them, probably the most obvious ones. Could I share a little of your expertise about risk? I mean if there are some risks that are easily forgotten.'

'Yes, there are two types of risk that are obvious when explained, but nevertheless quite often neglected. I'm thinking of systematic and non-systematic risk. It's often easier to explain these risks by starting with non-systematic risk. I would say that non-systematic risk is the risk that affects companies differently, or rather some companies but not others. Take, for example, a company manufacturing ice cream. This company is heavily influenced by the weather. Good weather will result in good sales and share prices are likely to go up, whereas a bad summer is likely to lead to bad sales figures that may cause the share price to go down. However, the bad weather wouldn't lead to a general stock market decline.

'The other type of risk, systematic risk, is a measurement of an individual share's sensitivity to changes in the whole market. Suppose a company sees its shares change by 1.5%, when the market, generally expressed by a broad market index such as the Market100, changes by say 1%; this company is oversensitive. If you'll allow me to be slightly technical, you would say that that particular company has a beta of 1.5. A beta value of 1 means the share changes in line with the market and a beta value of 0.5 means the company is undersensitive to changes in the market. You've got to bear in mind that these beta values are based on historical data and they have to be considered as such.

'In portfolio theory the likelihood of portfolios developing in line with the beta value is greater as the number of companies increases. Empirical studies show that at least 15 different shares increase that probability significantly. At the same time, by increasing the number of different shares – and I think 15 is becoming some sort of magical number in this sense – you also reduce the non-systematic risk, unless all 15 are in the same business. One way to reduce the non-systematic risk of holding shares in the ice cream company could be to buy shares in a company organising holiday trips abroad. With bad weather there should be a healthy growth in the sales of holiday trips abroad. On that subject, bad weather or not, I'd love to see the whole family up with me in Vermont before too long. You know there is an open invitation and I'll get the opportunity to teach Edward and James how to catch the really big fish.' Ben finished and took a sip of port.

'What about credit risk then?' I said.

'Well, there is always an element of credit risk involved in equities. That's why you should expect a higher compensation than from a risk-free investment. The way to reduce credit risk is, funnily enough, done through diversification. By increasing the number of different shares in the portfolio to around the magic number of 15, you're killing two birds with one stone – reducing the non-systematic risk as I said before and also the credit risk. However, the best way of reducing the credit risk or the risk of including an underperforming stock in your portfolio is to study the available accounts and statements, the annual report and other public information. If you think the price and the profit expectations for a company are too high, then simply avoid it.'

That was very useful. Diversification of the portfolio seemed to be the answer to eliminate or at least significantly reduce some rather nasty risks – systematic, non-systematic and credit risks.

## 14 June 2000

I had lunch with Mick Brown, chief economist at GlobalBank. It's good to keep the old network going. Anyway, he went through some theory behind currencies, which explained why they change and how it matters to a country and companies in that country.

He gave me an example. It was a bit basic and I think it went like this. Let's start with two countries – both being equal in terms of natural resources, production capacity, population, interest rates and everything else – we call the countries Happyland and Sadland. In Happyland people enjoyed working and they invented new ways to manufacture goods, which led to lower production costs. In Sadland, however, people were a bit lazy and wanted bells and whistles attached to many things in life.

Whilst Happyland could produce more goods at a lower cost, things in Sadland went the other way. They produced fewer goods at a higher cost. People in Sadland wanted to have more, and when they found out they had to pay more for the goods they bought from Happyland, they either had to stop buying these goods or reduce consumption of home-made goods. As a consequence, the shops in Sadland had to pay more for the goods from Happyland and to be able to do that they needed to exchange more saddollars for happydollars. The demand for saddollars shrunk and that was not something the government liked, because they were getting poorer and poorer. In order to compensate the situation, prices started to go up in Sadland.

Everything they had to buy from Happyland – from materials to finished goods – was now more expensive. As a result, the goods made in Sadland became more expensive. However, the situation in Happyland was just that – happy. For the same amount of money they could buy more goods, especially those imported from Sadland, and production materials from Sadland became cheaper, leading to lower costs and prices for the goods produced in Happyland. Now things obviously weren't the same in the two countries. Things were worse in Sadland and better in Happyland, but not all things. As the saddollar fell, people in Sadland stopped buying Happyland goods, because they were too expensive and people in Happyland bought more and more Sadland goods, because they were getting cheaper. The government in Sadland didn't like the situation with the falling saddollar, and in order to bring back some interest in the currency they hiked interest rates.

In Happyland the manufacturers started to complain over the strong currency, because their goods were losing attraction. Production started to fall and the government was urged to lower interest rates, but the government was hesitant. Why was that? Well, because they were concerned about the mounting consumption in Happyland. Higher consumption meant higher demand, and higher demand meant higher prices. The government wanted to make consumption less attractive and one way of doing that is to increase interest rates. So what will happen next? Higher interest rates in Sadland, but not in Happyland may bring the decline of the saddollar to an end and may also see it strengthen a bit. Higher interest rates in both countries may result in a continued strengthening of the happydollar (and decline of the saddollar) and in fact an acceleration of that trend. To see unchanged interest rates in both countries is very unlikely, and so is higher interest rates in Happyland only.

Currency risk is all about changes in the relationship between two or more currencies. Things in the real world are certainly more complex, and expectations come into play to make them even more complex. With expectations, people are not waiting to see something happen; rather, if they believe something is likely to happen, they will act accordingly. Mike's final word of wisdom was, 'When you're managing currency risk, you're effectively trying to anticipate, not just what is going to happen, but also what people – the market – are expecting to happen.'

It means that when investing in shares with other currency denominations, I must not only analyse the company in question but also form a view of the currency and, more importantly, how that currency is likely to develop in relation to the pound. Even if the company does well and the share price goes up, I may get beaten by a depreciation of the currency.

## 17 June 2000

Weekend at last, not that it matters a lot to me, but Edward and James not having to go to school gave an excellent opportunity to take the boys up to London. It was a lovely summer's day. The boys like going by train, so we settled for that. We took the train to Victoria and jumped on a bus to Covent Garden. We started off at the Transport Museum, followed by lunch at a nearby hamburger place. Then we made our way down to Leicester Square to watch a film. We agreed on *Tarzan*, and it was very entertaining. On the way out I bumped into Roger Smith, an old schoolmate of mine, who is now, would you believe it, in asset management with Smith Brothers. I asked him if he could teach me some tricks of the trade at a later stage, which he said he'd be happy to. (His name Smith has nothing to do with Smith Brothers – it's just a coincidence.)

## 19 June 2000

In all a very good weekend. Lots of time with the boys and very nice weather helped. Back to my risk studies, Today I explored two more risks. By the way, I've decided they are the final two I will bother with at this stage – liquidity risk and asymmetric risk.

I want to know about liquidity risk so I can meet all my payments on time and understand the characteristics of all the money flows – money in and money out.

Asymmetric risk is best explained by an example I found in a book. In a business deal, one party has made an offer that the other party is now considering. He has the right to accept, but no obligation to do so. If it is a fixed-price offer and market prices go up, the offer will become more attractive to the second party, who is now likely to accept. The first party is facing a rather bad deal, given the new circumstances. The risk in this deal situation is asymmetric, because the first party is bound by the offer and exposed to changes in the market and their impact on the value of the offer, whereas the other party has no risk, just an opportunity. All risk sits with the first party. Very much like an option contract, which is another good example of asymmetric risk. The buyer of an option contract is given the right, but not the obligation, to exercise the contract, whereas the writer of the option contract has the obligation to exercise the contract, when called upon to do so.

I will have to come back to risk at a later stage – how to measure it and manage it. For now, I am happy to understand that I know more about risks and that I must try to avoid the beast of beasts – risk risk.

## 20 June 2000

The risk exercise I just did was good, not least because I must ensure that my fund management system can support the way I want to trade, and measure risk and performance. I'm not quite in a position to rubber-stamp my approach yet, because there are several things I want to go over before I come to measure risk and performance. One of them is natural hedges. When talking about natural hedges, it's about cyclical and contracyclical shares, or indeed other shares that react and counter-react to external factors, cancelling each other out. However important that is, I think I need to define those other external factors which are worth considering and I should try to identify shares and companies, or indeed other possible instruments, that will help me address any changes in them. I know about the Greeks and I know what derivatives are sensitive to, but now I want to examine potential factors that may impact share prices generally. One such factor is interest rates. Others are weather, currencies and economic cycles. An example for weather is the ice cream company and the travel company, but I need to do a thorough examination of the stock market and see what live examples there are. This table's a good starting point

| Cyclical shares | Non-cyclical shares |
|---|---|
| Cars | Food and drugs |
| Household goods | Beverages |
| Leisure and entertainment | Health |
| Media | Tobacco |
| Restaurants and pubs | Telecommunication services |
| Transport | |

I contacted my old friend Alan James, who works for Lifestyle Asset Management, to arrange a meeting on betas and more generally the key development trends in the asset management industry. He agreed to a lunch date in mid-July. Should be good to see him again.

## 22 June 2000

Trouble, trouble and more trouble. Fortunately, it wasn't about business. The kitchen sink was completely blocked. When considering how to attack the problem, I first thought of the old hands-on methods, but because I've a three-plughole sink, I decided to go for chemical warfare. It had always worked well in the past, so I couldn't see why it wouldn't work this time. I found some sink and plughole unblocker. It seemed to be pretty straightforward – no mention of protective clothing, gloves or goggles. Down it went, and after an hour's wait it was time to test whether I'd been successful. It wasn't exactly 100% sorted, but the flow down the drain was significantly improved.

This sink exercise took me all the way up to lunch and I gradually felt another day had been lost. I decided to do some web research, but it wasn't very successful. I had to register for most of the sites I wanted to visit. I did it but the approval isn't granted instantly. I'll check again tomorrow to see if I've been given access.

## 23 June 2000

I got up early to go to the office. A quick breakfast and off I went. I'd just drunk a cup of coffee with Caroline when my mobile phone rang. It was Amanda, and she was seriously annoyed because the kitchen sink was blocked again. I said I'd have another go when I got home, but she couldn't wait that long. She decided to ask Andre, our neighbour, for advice.

I settled down and began to surf the web again. I was more successful this time. Although I felt comfortable with what I saw, there wasn't much sign of betas. Most funds were tracking an index, either an official market index like the Market100 or an index calculated by one of the big investment banks. The latter provided global as well as 'regional' indices like a European index. I had a feeling that index tracking was all about picking a number of securities which, when taken together, have a similar development to the index itself. What were the possible ways of selecting securities to make up a portfolio that would track an index? I felt an urge to check this with Alan James.

## 24 June 2000

By now the blocked sink was a mystery. Nothing seemed to be good enough to help. We called the plumber and after some hours of digging around, he said the problem was tree roots. Apparently the big bayleaf tree had grown beyond belief. He cut the roots back, but that was only a temporary solution. The tree had to be taken down.

## 18 July 2000

After a few weeks off I now need to look at how to measure my performance. I suppose it's easy to determine whether you've gained or lost money, but what does it tell me? Could I have made or lost more money on alternative investments? If the market goes down and I don't sell, I haven't realised any losses. I've only lost value and it might come back again. Or should I regard lost value as a realised loss? Consequently, when the market goes up, must I sell to benefit from the increase in value to realise a profit? What is the difference, if any, between realised profits and losses on the one hand and rise and fall in value on the other hand?

First of all I need to determine how to measure performance. These days it seems that most asset and fund management firms measure their performance against an index – a benchmark of some sort. I need to understand the theory behind replicating indices and the benefits of measuring against benchmarks. I mean, if the benchmark has a negative performance one year, would my clients be happy to see my fund do the same? How, if measuring against a benchmark, can you differentiate yourself? Surely, just trying to do what the benchmark – the market – is doing can't be enough to attract investors.

This is something else I need to discuss with Alan James when we meet for lunch later today. He's been in the asset management business for a long time and he should be able to help me with answers to my questions.

Unfortunately, I had to postpone the lunch, but while I was on the phone, I told him that I'd left GlobalBank and that I was in the middle of setting up my own fund management business: 'I've come across some issues I'd like to discuss with you.'

'Thomas, you know I'm always happy to help as long as you leave my clients alone. What would you like to discuss?'

'Don't you worry,' I reassured him, 'You've got institutional clients and I'm after clients like you and me. The idea I have is to use derivatives to enhance portfolio performance and to be more fleet-footed. The big question is how I should measure performance.'

'The name of the game these days is benchmarking. You measure performance against a benchmark, which could be a market index of some sort. There are, as you well know, official indices such as the Market100. On top of that you have the investment banks calculating a whole range of wider indices, like global market and global industry indices. GlobalBank used to be pretty good at that, right? Anyway, depending on your investment strategy, you have to pick a benchmark accordingly. For example, if the UK stock market is your market, Market100 would be a good benchmark.'

'Yes, well I kind of grasp that, but what value do I add by replicating Market100? It's not exactly unique, is it? And how can I incorporate the use of derivatives in this context?'

'When you look at the overall market portfolio – in this example, all companies making up Market100 – you can do that by considering a number of different risk measures akin to those for options – volatility for example. You know I'm sales director, so don't expect me to go too deep into technicalities but, as an example, if you can replicate Market100 with less risk in terms of volatility, your portfolio's performance should be more consistent than Market100. On average they should be the same, but the swings in performance in Market100 would be greater. Sometimes it would outperform your portfolio and sometimes it would underperform. To some investors that's worth quite a lot.'

'Do all the individual investments have to be in constituents of the index or could you go outside that scope?'

'No, I don't think they have to, but I'll double-check for you if you wish. I think the important thing is that your core investment is in line with the benchmark. It just wouldn't make sense otherwise and you would expose yourself to substantial risks. For example, if you picked the Japanese Market100 as your benchmark and you only invested in UK Market100 companies, you would be seriously exposed. And I doubt your investors would approve of that set-up.'

That reassured me.

## 19 July 2000

One issue remaining and that's the accounting. I'll have to check with Tim (my accountant). There could be a difference in how to account for realised profits and losses arising from derivatives, as opposed to unrealised (value changes only) in the underlying. From a portfolio viewpoint I'll treat them equally, but I must understand the implications for my year-end accounts. Surely there must be an industry standard. Whichever way, people must be able to compare my performance with that of other fund managers.

# CHAPTER FIVE

## 11 October 2000

I thought it could be good to keep track of some key developments. Obviously, how the business is developing is important as well as to check hours of sleep and time for the family. I'll try to start each entry by keeping track of six items:

| | |
|---|---|
| New clients | Total funds to manage |
| Time home | Fund performance |
| Sleep hours | Market100 (level, change) |

BIG QUESTION How to get clients? The 'campaign' isn't due for another two weeks. Must be something we can do in the meantime. But what?

Arrived at the office to find Caroline bouncing up and down shouting, 'Our first client, our first client, hurrah, hurrah!' I joined in but I had to stop her after a while to hear what it was all about.

'He came through the letterbox – the cheque that is. A cheque for £500 000 to be invested in Fund1,' Caroline giggled.

'Jolly good! Champagne again,' I yelled.

After lunch I sat down and thought about how to establish a balanced exposure while building up the fund. The strategy was clear – I had to use derivatives. I decided to invest the funds in the most interesting companies and balance this with futures/options on the Market100 index in combination with long call options/short put options on underinvested companies.

## 24 October 2000

Another good day at the office. Some more clients, which is a good indicator that my fellow board members are taking it with enthusiasm. I thought it'd be nice for the family to get away on holiday together. This year has been all about building the business and no time for things like that. Maybe Easter time next year is a good opportunity. I must start to look at possible places to visit. Christmas is coming up in two months and the big marketing campaign is on the horizon, so this side of New Year is out of the question.

## 25 October 2000

*New clients 7 – total funds to manage £575 000, Market100 up 0.38 to 100.75 – time home yesterday 7pm – hours of sleep 6.5 good*

I've been focusing on the marketing campaign, which is going live today. Really nerve-racking! Nice day today. I'll try to make it an early finish and take the family out for dinner. I know the boys have homework and all that, but they've been doing really well this year and I'm sure Amanda wouldn't mind an evening away from the cooker.

## 10 November 2000

*New clients massive 25 – total funds up to £1.2 million – Market100 stable at 100.78 – time home yesterday 4pm – did the restaurant and worked out very well – hours in bed amazing 8 (hours of sleep significantly less)*

Got to the office around 9am. Called Don to let him know the campaign seemed to be spot on. The campaign is going to run for another three weeks, which will take us just up to the beginning of December.

Today I decided to have a closer look at market fundamentals and whether there are any strong trends in the market. I've been focusing all my attention on setting up the business and it's about time I started to focus on the investment side of things. This year the market's been fairly quiet – Market100 has risen by a modest 3.5%.

Phoned Ben in the afternoon. He wasn't around, so I left him a message that the campaign was off to a flyer.

Phoned some banks and asked them to send their economic outlooks and newsletters on equities. Had a chance to chat with Mick Brown at GlobalBank again. His view was that next year would probably see a stable growth in GDPs around the world, and companies would most likely continue to show good profits and growth prospects. He felt the equities markets might rise a bit more than this year, maybe by 10–12%. He identified some key factors for next year's markets. One was the value of the euro, which has been under pressure ever since the launch. Another was the slightly unrealistic valuation of dotcom and internet start-ups, which had taken the whole IT sector a lot higher already. It's not unlikely it could continue to rally well into next year. Or was it going to prove a more realistic valuation? Tricky!

Spent the rest of the afternoon looking for Christmas presents and thought about the fact that next year I'd have to come up with something brilliant to give to all my faithful and hopefully, by then, very pleased clients.

## 7 December 2000

Snapshot – the campaign's been a success with total funds just exceeding £5 million. The market has continued to be quiet, which has suited me. Still unclear where the market's going, which means I've kept building Fund1 by investing in equities, but so far I haven't been using derivatives.

Another board meeting coming up in a week's time. It calls for serious celebration. At the same time it would be good to be in a position to disclose my first derivatives position. I have a feeling all the uncertainty and the fact that the market's been so quiet for the last two months is giving rise to an opportunity for strategies based on undecided markets with increasing volatility – we're talking about long straddle or long strangle. Since 5% of the fund value is held in cash, I would have £250 000 available for derivatives. However, I won't go for full blast now. Need to test my wings first.

It's hard to think it's Christmas in a few weeks time. Amanda's already done the Advent decorations and now the boys are pestering us to go ahead and buy the Christmas tree. In my family we've always been a bit out of phase in the sense we've not taken it in and decorated it until the weekend before Christmas. My dad spent a few winters in Sweden during the early fifties and that's probably where he picked up the tradition. However, we keep the Christmas tree longer after Christmas. Again, according to the Swedish tradition, the Christmas tree is thrown out on 13 January with some sort of plunder for the tree party – great for kids! Anyway, got to focus on the business now.

I loaded the options calculator and started to toy around. It was a long straddle I wanted to check out. I entered all the fields I had to in order to trigger the calculation – underlying price, which is the current market price 100.25, the strike price 100, volatility 15%, interest rate 5% and days to expiry, in this case 104 (March contract). The resulting call price was 4.0756 and the put price was 2.4111. So what does this mean then?

Well, each contract (unit of trading) is valued at £10 per index point, so if I want to buy 500 contracts, I will have to pay PREMIUM × NUMBER OF CONTRACTS × 10. The cost of the call options would be £20 378 and the cost of the put options £12 056. In total I would have to pay £32 434.

I phoned Derivatives Brokers to discuss the idea. They were of course keen to do business, but said there was little in the current market indicating a major market movement. I thought that was slightly encouraging, since it meant volatility had to be low and possibly expectations even lower, which in all would mean options were cheaper, all other things being equal.

However, I wasn't 100% sure whether to go ahead with the strategy. At the same time I knew I had to act soon to take advantage of the quiet market and to avoid the end of the year, which invariably results in all sorts of anomalies in terms of funding rates and asset prices. The willingness to trade and to take on positions was dropping rapidly.

I'm off to my first Christmas lunch now, so it'll have to wait until later. I'm looking forward to this lunch. For the last three years Tim, George and I have met up around Christmas and it's become a sort of tradition. Tim and George were among my best clients at GlobalBank. They might have some market insight to guide me in my decision. We'll see about that! Anyway, this year we'll meet at the George (yes he got to choose this year) on the south side. Apparently one of the oldest pubs in London. Should be fun.

Back from lunch. We had an interesting discussion about the markets and I think the conclusion was that you can make a strong case for higher as well as lower stock markets next year.

After some consideration I've finally made up my mind. I'll go ahead with the long straddle, which means buying equal numbers of call and put options at the same strike price for the same

| TRADE CONFIRMATION | |
|---|---|
| **CONTRACT** | MARCH 2001 (104 DAYS REMAINING) |
| **TYPE** | CALL |
| **TRANSACTION TYPE** | OPENING PURCHASE |
| **NO. OF CONTRACTS** | 500 |
| **STRIKE PRICE** | 100 |
| **UNDERLYING INDEX VALUE** | 100.25 |
| **CALL/PUT VALUE** | 4.0756 |
| **INTEREST RATE** | 5% |
| **VOLATILITY** | 15% |
| **TOTAL TO PAY/RECEIVE** | £20 378 PAY |

month (March 2001). I called Derivatives Brokers and gave them my order. Charles Smith called back shortly after and said the order had been executed. I felt relieved and thought that was enough work for the day. Asked Caroline to join me at the wine bar. This was a good cause for some champagne!

| TRADE CONFIRMATION | |
|---|---|
| **CONTRACT** | MARCH 2001 (104 DAYS REMAINING) |
| **TYPE** | PUT |
| **TRANSACTION TYPE** | OPENING PURCHASE |
| **NO. OF CONTRACTS** | 500 |
| **STRIKE PRICE** | 100 |
| **UNDERLYING INDEX VALUE** | 100.25 |
| **CALL/PUT VALUE** | 2.4111 |
| **INTEREST RATE** | 5% |
| **VOLATILITY** | 15% |
| **TOTAL TO PAY/RECEIVE** | £12 056 PAY |

## 8 December 2000

*Too much champagne yesterday! – Market100 pretty unchanged – still £5 million to look after – TGIF*

Today was an off day. Nothing much happened. Caroline and I made the final preparations for the board meeting on the 14th – next Thursday. The key points then will obviously be the success of the campaign and my first options strategy.

## 12 December 2000

*Still no market movement – probably won't happen this side of New Year – Market100 at 99.98 – good night's sleep, horrendous train journeys both ways yesterday*

Every winter it's the same. Late-running services, cancellations and shorter trains than normal. It's because of the wrong type of leaves on the line, or the wrong type of snow, or some other bad excuse. What baffles me most is how any of this could have an impact on the number of carriages.

Business-wise, everything is in order for the board meeting. That's a relief! A bit concerned the market's still unchanged. It would have been really neat to show a bit of profit on the options, but I'll have to sell them the concept instead. Now, with no major movement, the time value is gradually creeping away.

I suppose I'll have to provide a fresh evaluation for the meeting.

## 14 December 2000

*Still no market movement to talk about – Market100 at 100.16 – everything else is okay – board meeting day*

The board meeting is due at 1pm today. I'll meet up with Ben at 11 o'clock to go through the agenda. Checked the value of the options this morning. It had fallen to £21 286. Volatility, which had fallen from 15% to 10%, and a further decline in time value were the main culprits.

The board meeting went well. Everyone was thrilled the marketing campaign had been so successful. Then I had the opportunity to explain what the options strategy was all about – to take advantage of a movement either way. A breakout from the dull market would lead to increased volatility, which would further boost the value of the options. The board shared my view with a bias the market was going higher in the next year. No one expected falling prices, but most expected modest gains. The question now was whether the market would move soon enough and significantly enough to make my strategy pay off.

What was more of a test was the 'risk inquisition' instigated by Greg. Greg, and the rest of the board, wanted me to prove I knew my stuff regarding risk, before giving the final go-ahead. 'So, Thomas,' he began, 'I believe it's been back to the world of theoretical finance for you over the last few months. We hope it's been useful and I know from my colleagues at GlobalBank that you've done a lot of work. I'm pleased you've been out and about in the market and apparently seeking opinions on the latest developments in the markets. I, or rather we, won't make you pass an exam but we do need to ensure that you know enough to start the business for real. Based on the investment strategy for Fund1 could you please explain to us what potential risks you'll face in the day-to-day business and how you intend to monitor and manage them.'

'Certainly, my dear friends. I will take some time to expand a bit on this then I'll show you some of the reports available from my fund management system, which I chose largely because of its excellent risk management tools. I've identified five categories of risk:

Over- or underexposure to Market100
Systematic and non-systematic risk
Credit risk (or default risk)
Currency risk
Derivatives risks – hedge risks and delta (speculative) risks

'Over- or underexposure to Market100 – the benchmark – is an obvious risk, since we do measure performance against the index, and deviation in correlation between the shares I'm holding and the Market100 index will register as over- or underperformance. I'm not intending to hold all the shares making up Market100, but rather a cross-section of shares that replicate the index. The replication will be based on historical data between the chosen shares and Market100. Nevertheless, since I'm not holding all the index constituents, some shares may diverge from their historical pattern, resulting in over- or underperformance of the fund. This will be monitored on a daily basis and the portfolio will be continuously rebalanced to eliminate this risk, unless of course it's a conscious decision, for example, to reduce exposure in a falling market.

'Systematic and non-systematic risks are chiefly managed by

the same tool, called diversification. Through keeping the portfolio diversified, which by nature it should be if it's to track the index, these risks are significantly reduced. Furthermore, by avoiding or replacing shares that are in the "risk zone" this should be a further tool to manage these risks. By "risk zone" I mean companies in a certain sector that have high exposure to certain events. I would either move away from the sector entirely or replace the shares for others in the same sector with lower exposure.

'Credit risk, as it happens, is also best avoided by diversification. Well, it's not avoided, but placing your eggs in more than one basket significantly reduces the impact of a default. I think the only other way of managing credit risk is by monitoring the companies – how they perform, what information they give and how the market reacts to it. I subscribe to corporate action data from one of the most well-respected companies in this area, as well as news clippings from relevant business media, which means I have early warning systems in place. Other than that, it's a matter of staying in touch with the market – listen to the gossip and all that.

'Currency risk is a different story. As a rule, I would hedge the currency component by agreeing the exchange rate for the reverse transaction through the forward market. If I hold my foreign currency shares during the same period as the currency hedge, there is no currency risk. However, if I hold the foreign currency shares for a shorter or longer period then the return is not certain, which is why I will take my position and continually mark it to market, even intra-day. Instead of selling shares ahead of plans, I can use put options or futures contracts in that market for the period up until the forward currency contract matures and the whole position can be unwound. Derivatives are an even neater way to gain exposure to companies and markets without currency risk, or at least with limited currency risk. Since the investment for a derivatives position is a fraction of the investment for a cash position with the same risk, the currency risk is lower. And that leads on to the fifth category, which I call derivatives risk.

'I've divided derivatives risk into two subgroups – one called hedge risk and the other delta or speculative risk. Hedge risk is the risk associated with premiums paid and the risk of losses due to adverse market movements or changes in market conditions that negatively impact long options positions. It's really a sub-risk of delta risks or overall alignment and performance in relation to the benchmark. Using all the Greeks, but primarily the delta, I'll monitor the development of any derivatives position separately and included in the overall portfolio. Really, it'll be simulations like this: What will be the outcome if X happens? I can measure theoretical performance if the market goes up or down, volatility rises or declines, interest rates are hiked or lowered, or any combination of these.

'To sum up, I would like to show you some reports which are examples of simulations – in this case if the market goes up by 5%, declines by 5% or stays the same. The next one has the same market scenarios, but now volatility is the variable. Two additional scenarios – volatility up 10% and volatility down 10%. Volatility unchanged is the same as the initial scenarios.

There are some other risk measures as well; one of the more well known is Value at Risk, or VaR. VaR, as you know, is based on historical volatility and used in isolation. In my opinion, it's a route to disaster. Why? Well, because if volatility keeps coming down, VaR will allow greater positions – greater exposure – and almost with certainty we know there will be a change in the market – the market will erupt up or down, if something can erupt down. The result – the falling volatility has allowed an increasing exposure that all of a sudden explodes in your face. VaR may have its merits if applied in conjunction with other measures, but not on its own. That's my view.'

'Very impressive, Thomas, very impressive indeed. I think I can speak for the whole board in saying I'm thoroughly reassured. The final go-ahead is hereby granted.' Greg was clearly satisfied.

The board went on to approve the strategy for Fund1. However, it had already been agreed and this was just a formality.

On remuneration of the board, the agreement was that a small fee would apply from the beginning of 2001 and that shares and options could be discussed early in 2002, after the first year's evaluation.

Rounded off with another Christmas lunch. Began with champagne in the office and carried on very much the same way.

## 30 December 2000

I've been having a lazy spell since the board meeting. It's been really good to have time for the boys and to do things with the family. I'm not going to spend many minutes on the diary today. I just want to record that Market100 ended the year at 100.00.

**Year-end summary**

| | |
|---|---|
| Market100 | 100.00 |
| Fund1 performance | +0.78% |
| Total funds | £5 500 000 |
| Shares | £5 225 000 |
| Cash | £242 566 |
| Derivatives | £32 434 (current value £18 447) |

Happy New Year!

## 2 January 2001

*Nothing exciting so far*

This is the time of year when all investment banks and gurus stick their necks out to predict the coming year in terms of stock market development among other things. A lacklustre last year seems to give hope for increasing markets this year. The most optimistic forecast is Market100 to gain 23%. The least optimistic is a gain of 7%, with an average of +14%. I hope they are right and that we can have an early rally, please.

Otherwise, my strategy for the year is to have a rather low marketing profile and focus on what I've got. Hopefully, towards the second half of the year I can show reasonable performance as evidence that I should acquire new funds more aggressively.

In terms of different industries and sectors, I think the technology sector needs a closer look. It took a hit towards the end of last year and some say it will continue to suffer, whereas others say it'll bounce back. Could be the key to it all!

The economy seems extremely healthy. Unemployment at low levels, inflation under control, interest rates at their peak and likely to edge lower, and a fair bit of public spending into healthcare and other similar sectors. On the negative side, there are signals from the US and Japan of slower economic growth, which has been met by cuts in interest rates. However, if the trend remains, the question is whether further cuts in interest rates will suffice to cheer up the stock markets. The dark horse is Europe.

Back from lunch. Pleased to see the market moving up – Market100 up 2.5% so far. The Asian markets did well overnight and the expectation is that the US markets will open higher as well.

## 3 January 2001

*Pleasing start – Market100 up 2.8% to 102.80 – slept very well last night – the old suit was a bit tight after the holidays, probably need to lose some weight, perhaps 1–2 stone*

The options strategy is beginning to go the right way. After yesterday's rise the value is now £30 003. The market is indicating a further rise today. Brilliant! It's coming back to me.

Although I'm pleased about the markets, I do feel pretty miserable. I think I've got the flu. Got to be an early night.

## 8 January 2001

*Market100 last week closed at 104.73, wonderful news – I've been tucked up in bed for most of the last five days, but starting to feel a bit better*

More hints and ideas in the business press on where the markets are going. Some gurus seem to favour non-cyclical sectors such as banks, insurance and drugs, since they are not sensitive to the swings of the economy, whereas cyclical sectors such as cars, steel and building materials are doomed to suffer as the economy tumbles. Something to bear in mind.

I can't get rid of the feeling there's a bubble about to burst. Private consumption is booming, house prices keep rising ridiculously and there's a widespread Klondike feeling. I mean, when cabbies start to give you investment advice it's time to be cautious. Genuine uncertainty! Oh, bloody headache, and for once it's got nothing to do with alcohol or hard thinking. Still the flu pestering me.

Since I'm working from home for a few more days, I called Caroline in the office to check that everything was okay. It was. Nothing much to attend to at all. It's gone really quiet during the holidays. I guess it'll pick up this week. Tony phoned last week and said the City was like a ghost town. No one around basically. You could walk into any pub or bar, go straight to the counter and order whatever you wanted – all five pairs of eyes glued on you. A bit scary.

I settled down with the business press and found more predictions for the coming year. On the positive side, oil prices have come off their peak, interest rates are likely to come down in the US and possibly in the UK – if the government plans an election this year – and any of the problems with the dotcoms seem to be dealt with.

On the negative side, the cost of corporate debt (the cost for companies to borrow money) has risen sharply, profit forecasts are down as well as credit ratings, especially in the telecoms sector, and the overall slowing down in the global economy has to be considered. Furthermore, if large share positions are funded by borrowed money, forced selling could add to a negative trend. Finally, more mention of value stocks, i.e. non-cyclicals.

Later I had a look through some useful web pages and to my surprise I found some advice praising cyclical shares. Confusion is total. Goodnight.

## 12 January 2001

*Market100 at 103.75, down a bit since my last entry – volatility up to 20% – finally got rid of the flu*

Positive signal – the Fed lowered rates by 0.25%. I bet the market's going to jump for joy today.

Yes, righty-ho. Market100 closed at 106.52. The US Market100 was up 1.15%. Great!

## 12 February 2001

*Market100 at 107.27 – now we're talking*

Lots of work lately with our clients, their accounts and year-end statements. Caroline's doing a great job.

Options, yes options. I'm considering closing my long straddle, at least the call leg. If I believe the market is going down from here then that would be a great idea, but I'm not certain it will. Not soon enough anyway.

Phoned Charles at Derivatives Direct for some advice. I felt even more uncertain after that chat, so I decided to close the whole position. Since volatility had risen to 27%, even the put options were doing reasonably well, considering a bull market. I closed it. Market100 stood at 107.23.

| TRADE CONFIRMATION | |
|---|---|
| **CONTRACT** | MARCH 2001 (40 DAYS REMAINING) |
| **TYPE** | PUT |
| **TRANSACTION TYPE** | CLOSING SALE |
| **NO. OF CONTRACTS** | 500 |
| **STRIKE PRICE** | 100 |
| **UNDERLYING INDEX VALUE** | 107.23 |
| **CALL/PUT VALUE** | 0.6313 |
| **INTEREST RATE** | 5% |
| **VOLATILITY** | 27% |
| **TOTAL TO PAY/RECEIVE** | £3157 RECEIVE |

| TRADE CONFIRMATION | |
|---|---|
| **CONTRACT** | MARCH 2001 (40 DAYS REMAINING) |
| **TYPE** | CALL |
| **TRANSACTION TYPE** | CLOSING SALE |
| **NO. OF CONTRACTS** | 500 |
| **STRIKE PRICE** | 100 |
| **UNDERLYING INDEX VALUE** | 107.23 |
| **CALL/PUT VALUE** | 8.2305 |
| **INTEREST RATE** | 5% |
| **VOLATILITY** | 27% |
| **TOTAL TO PAY/RECEIVE** | £41 153 RECEIVE |

Net on the first options strategy I gained £11 876. Very good indeed!

## 16 February 2001

*Market100 at 108.61, would you believe it? – nothing seems to stop the rally – did I close the straddle too soon? – he who lives will see*

Is the rally going to continue? Is it well founded? I'm not certain. Probably best to be on the sideline for a while until new signals are available.

## 23 February 2001

*Market100 at 105.47, down from its high of 108.62, but no significant change in sentiment – probably a bit of profit taking – market sentiment still very positive*

Spoke with Greg today. There seems to be more money coming into the market all the time. Market sentiment is still generally bullish. I personally think there are some strange valuations of dotcoms and internet start-ups compared to traditional companies. A lot of it is wishful thinking, and price/earnings ratios seem a bit high in many cases. I have a bearish feeling, but it may still be a bit too soon. Volatility is still high at 25% and I need to consider the alternatives carefully. To establish a long put option position may cost me a lot in premium outlay if the market move I anticipate doesn't happen; whereas short call options come with limited earnings potential if I'm right, and a greater risk of losing money if I'm wrong.

I need to develop a view as to how much I think the market can fall by. If it's a significant fall then outright put options may be right, whereas a slow and not so significant movement is better met by other strategies.

## 2 March 2001

*Market100 at 105.24, still positive – no, I haven't lost any weight – need to do some exercise I guess – drink fewer pints, possibly – sleeping well, so far so good with the business and the idea of being home not too late and all that*

I'm starting to build my own scenario, which in essence is that the market movements this year will be within a band ranging from 110 at the top end and 95 at the bottom. This means at current market levels there's roughly a 10% potential to the bottom and a further 5% to the top. I say potential in terms of a decline, since this is where I see derivatives being most useful this year. So far, I haven't been able to identify any opportunities for derivatives in terms of individual companies or industries.

I need to develop my strategy accordingly, but I have a feeling that the March contract is to close in time. And until it has expired, the time value of the June contract is too high. I'll have to wait until the end of March or the beginning of April to make my next move.

## 9 March 2001

*Market100 at 106.04, up a bit – only a week left until the March contracts expire – good last week (starting to see the sun again)*

My ambition to lose some weight hasn't been met too successfully. This morning I decided to pop out and buy new scales for the office. (I think the ones at home have been lying.)

I've had a busy week meeting investment bankers and economists. The bankers wanted to sell various ideas and packages, but they were either away from my core business or too complex. The economists were a more useful bunch of people for my intents and purposes. They confirmed the slowing down in the US economy and that the UK and euro-zone economies were still doing quite well. The interest rate cuts by the Fed have been good for the markets, but whether it'll be enough for all of this year is another question. Just wait and see what the outcome and the interpretation of the first company interim reports will be.

Caroline has just sent out the stuff for this year's first board meeting to be held on 5 April. I'll have my new derivatives strategy thought through by then. Be good to have their views and reactions.

## 16 March 2001

*Expiry day for the March contracts, which closed at 106.53*

The March contracts have gone. Lucky I didn't have any positions left. The final stages of the market were really volatile and there were attempts to push the market higher. Obviously huge money at stake, so it seems rational to throw in a few more bobs and try to have your position close in the money. However, it rarely works, because the market forces work both ways, i.e. the other side of the positions would naturally want the market to close lower. Anyway, the exchange officials normally have the power to overrule obvious attempts at market manipulation.

What a day yesterday! It started as a quiet pint on the way home and ended up at closing time. There was some sort of get-together for old colleagues from GlobalBank. After a few, Greg turned up and began a wee bit of serious discussion, but then we just had a really good time, like in the old days. Being on my own, that's something I miss – the team spirit and good fun. By sitting in a dealing room full of action and racing pulses, I invariably got ideas and inspiration for new deals and proposals. Now it's all down to me to make contact with people and initiate a sensible discussion. Maybe I should expand the company a bit, take on one or two new staff to boost the level of activity in the office. I suppose it would make sense to have some sort of back-up if I'm away. Caroline will definitely take on greater responsibilities, but she doesn't fit the bill yet. I should probably find someone rather senior as my deputy and a new assistant; this might open the way for Caroline to focus more on sales and customer management.

The phone's ringing. Bye for now.

## 30 March 2001

*Market100 at 104.66, down – is this the beginning of a declining market or just a small reaction? – no, I haven't lost any weight – gained 2lb instead*

Although the economist J M Keynes wasn't one of my favourites, he once said, 'There's only one thing in life I regret and that is not drinking more champagne.' I, on the other hand, seem to be doing my best not to repeat that mistake. Another infamous wine bar do earlier this week. This time organised by some consultants. Steve Alexander invited me, and the theme for the night was business continuity planning; it seemed more like champagne continuity planning.

My strategy is coming together.

## 6 April 2001

*Market100 at 106.75, up again – board meeting yesterday – went very well*

**End of March summary**

| **Current position** | **Invested** | **Value** |
|---|---|---|
| Shares | 5 225 000 | 5 577 688 |
| Cash | 286 866* | 290 359 |
| Options | 0 | 0 |
| Total value | 5 511 866 | 5 868 047 |
| Total growth | 11 866 (+0.21%) | 368 047 (+6.69%) |

* Includes options profit/loss

Not too bad, not too bad at all – compared to Market100 being 6.75% up. I'm happy with the result. Got to check how the other fund managers have fared though.

The essence of my overall strategy is to play within a band of Market100 of 110 to 95. The current level of 106 offers a limited upside, but a potentially bigger downside. Fundamentally, in terms of the economy and price/earnings ratios as well as the level of private debt, I'm actually quite bearish. I will therefore ignore the upside in terms of derivatives plays. I will focus on the downside. There are two key ways of playing the market. One is to buy put options and the other is to write call options. Both would be appropriate, but put options would have greater potential in a heavy fall. Market declines always happen faster and more dramatically than market rises. It's like a steam train pulling hard to reach the top of the hill, just to find that the track ends there and a steep fall takes over. A combination of the two would bring premium income from the written call options, which could be spent on premiums for the put options. The current level of volatility is 20%, which is reasonable, and short-term interest rates are still 5%. I'm willing to use £50 000 for premiums (less than 1% of initial fund value). This is for outright purchase of put options. Any premiums for written call options may be added to that, but they'll have to be assessed as and when they come into play, and they'll come into play when the anticipated market move hasn't occurred and written call options can add or replace the outright put options as part of the strategy.

The board were all up for the idea. I'll gradually edge into the position.

I briefly mentioned the idea that long term – I liked the way I put it – it may be necessary to take on new staff. I praised Caroline and said I wanted to secure her professional development, but that it has to be step by step. I continued to explain the need for a deputy, and with Caroline refocusing, the need for a new assistant.

Generally, the board agreed with what I said. Some useful comments, especially from Don. He said it's important to consolidate the business, take it step by step if you wish.

I won't do anything before the summer and it's probably a good idea to discuss things again at the August board meeting.

## 13 April 2001

*Market100 at 105.12 – otherwise pretty unchanged*

First I've engaged into the options market again. Bought some put options at 105.06 today. Just spent £14 897 on premiums. I'll keep watching the market, but I must say there's still little sign of any change in sentiment.

| TRADE CONFIRMATION | |
|---|---|
| **CONTRACT** | JUNE 2001 (63 DAYS REMAINING) |
| **TYPE** | PUT |
| **TRANSACTION TYPE** | OPENING PURCHASE |
| **NO. OF CONTRACTS** | 500 |
| **STRIKE PRICE** | 105 |
| **UNDERLYING INDEX VALUE** | 105.06 |
| **CALL/PUT VALUE** | 2.9793 |
| **INTEREST RATE** | 5% |
| **VOLATILITY** | 20% |
| **TOTAL TO PAY/RECEIVE** | £14 897 PAY |

Spent the last few days putting the Scalectrix track together. The boys got some new cars and some extension packs for their birthdays. It's awesome! It's got bridges and crossover tracks as well as a pit-stop stretch. Good fun!

## 20 April 2001

*Market100 at 105.38 – fewer pints actually, and I feel marginally slimmer – got a bit of stick this week – late home twice – tired now when Friday comes*

I'm just in the middle of arranging a surprise holiday for Amanda and myself. A week on our own in Tuscany should be good. Amanda's parents have promised to come and look after the boys. I wonder if they know what they're getting into. Nevertheless, I'm pleased and I'm sure James and Edward will feel the same when I break the news. Amanda should also be pleased and relieved they are in good hands. It's actually the first time we're going away on our own. One week isn't that long.

I extended my put option position by adding another £13 399 to the previous. I managed to get them near to the closing price at 105.36.

| TRADE CONFIRMATION | |
|---|---|
| CONTRACT | JUNE 2001 (54 DAYS REMAINING) |
| TYPE | PUT |
| TRANSACTION TYPE | OPENING PURCHASE |
| NO. OF CONTRACTS | 500 |
| STRIKE PRICE | 105 |
| UNDERLYING INDEX VALUE | 105.36 |
| CALL/PUT VALUE | 2.6798 |
| INTEREST RATE | 5% |
| VOLATILITY | 20% |
| TOTAL TO PAY/RECEIVE | £13 399 PAY |

## 27 April 2001

*Market100 at 104.39, going the right way – no significant change in market sentiment though – still fairly optimistic – would you believe it, I've lost 2lb – the weight I gained earlier in the year – back to square one*

I've decided to stick with the position I've got now and wait until I'm back from Tuscany to add to it, if the market is favourable enough, that is.

I can't say anything except that it's extraordinary how the market has gone flat like it did towards the end of last year. The only difference now is that the volatility is slightly higher. The market swings in a wider band. Without my strategy, I'd have gone for a long straddle or a long strangle, but now I can 'avoid' the outlay on the call options. If, big if, I'm right, that is. If the market goes up, I may wish I'd actually done the odd straddles or strangles, but here we are and I'm not going to change my mind.

## 4 May 2001

*Market100 at 106.21 – what's going on?*

Flying off to Pisa tomorrow and need some reassurance the market isn't going to rally. Phoned my old City contacts and they confirmed the market felt pretty strong, but unlikely to rally in the near future. Early June was going to be a first indicator, when some rather significant interim reports were due out. Anyway, I felt fine. My biggest concern should be a falling market rather than a bull market, since I haven't yet finalised my position. If the market goes up, I can carry on building my position at a lower cost.

The in-laws have just arrived. Won't be much time to do any more work until I'm back from holiday.

## 13 May 2001

*Market100 at 104.98, lower – but still the market's full of confidence – gained 4lb according to the home scales – unfortunately they've been fairly consistent with the scales I bought for the office*

It was a brilliant time in Tuscany. Flew into Pisa and rented a car to go to San Gimignano. I'd booked a room in an old farm-house outside the town, which had been converted to a modern and very charming hotel. Our room, they said when I booked, would be special, but nothing more than that. We had to wait and see. After the initial awkwardness of a left-hand drive car on the 'wrong' side of the road, we made rapid progress to the hotel.

We were well received and invited on a guided tour of the premises a bit later. When I got the room key I became a bit suspicious, because there was no room number on the key; it just said 'La Torre'. I asked if I'd got the right key, which I had. This was apparently the most spectacular room in the hotel. 'La Torre' was a room in a tower. Bathroom and a small lounge as you entered the room and a flight of stairs that took you up to the bedroom. It was a square room with windows in all directions and, most impressively, a view of San Gimignano itself.

San Gimignano has a characteristic skyline, with its high bell towers giving it the look of Manhattan. Actually, someone said that San Gimignano was the inspiration for Manhattan. Anyway, the bell towers date back to the thirteenth century at least, and it was said that families 'measured' fame and fortune by trying to build the highest bell tower. Of all those that were built, only twenty-odd have remained.

The hotel had a superb restaurant and an outdoor pool; we stayed by the pool on several days. Good food and trips to Florence and Venice were other highlights of a wonderful week. In terms of wine, the locally produced white wine Vernaccia di San Gimignano was very nice with seafood, whereas the absolute highlight was a red wine called Sassicaia. Sassicaia is made from the grape Cabernet Sauvignon, which is a very unusual grape in Tuscany. Hence the wine was not classified, but plainly labelled as table wine, which by no means should be taken literally. We couldn't resist buying a few cases to bring back home, since it must be among the best wines we've ever come across.

Phoned Caroline a few times, but nothing of great importance had occurred; that gave us more time and energy to focus on a truly splendid holiday.

## 18 May 2001

*Market100 at 105.29 – family life was very good last week – batteries recharged and full of energy to build my case for markets going down*

I had good conversations with George, Greg, Tim and a few of my economist friends. The outcome of these discussions is a table of positive and negative signs.

| Positive signs | Negative signs |
|---|---|
| More money coming into the market | Bond markets still outperforming major stock markets |
| UK election – keep the economy going, government wouldn't want to see higher interest rates | UK election – pre-election spending may lead to stable or even higher interest rates to curb inflationary pressure |
| More interest rate cuts to come in the US | Signals of lower consumer confidence in the US – further slowing of the ecomony |
| Technology sector took a beating last year – some signals it may have been an overreaction | Still very few internet start-ups that meet expectations – running into a shortage of funds |

On balance, it looks as if the positive signs are slightly stronger than the negative signs, but quite a few of them are ambiguous – they could go either way depending on the sentiment. Take UK interest rates for example. If they stay put or even head downwards, from a bullish viewpoint this would lead to lower cost of capital and increased levels of activity in the economy, boosting the stock market. However, lower interest rates may imply that the pound could be in for a tumble. For overseas investors, this may counter any stock market gains or actually erase any gains. Long-term, lower interest rates should be good for the stock markets, but short-term they could have the opposite impact.

It might be that the overall economy isn't slowing that badly, but rather there's a shift in expectations. Expectations are currently set very high in terms of sales and profit growth in most sectors. In the short term, a swing to more modest expectations may be bad news for the stock markets. Why? Well, I think for example that once there are new signals of a cooling off in terms of company sales and profit growth, the market is going to take a hit. This will lead to an awakening. The flow of liquidity out of shares into bonds will get a renewed boost. However, I don't expect a bottomless pit, but rather a normalisation, whatever that is.

## 25 May 2001

*Market100 at 106.59 – some discipline and a bit of exercise has paid off – 2lb lower*

When I close my eyes I see crocodiles, time crocodiles, eating away the value of my options. Maybe I've been wrong all the time about a fall in the market. Instead of a breakout, the market has narrowed and volatility has fallen. The right strategy would have been a short straddle or a short strangle, both of which would have benefited from lower volatility and time shortening.

I don't know how to act now. Should I do more things in the June contract, write the calls and buy some more puts or just write the calls? What if I was wrong then and the market starts to climb? Could be a nasty double whammy – losing on the initial put options as well as the written call options. Damn, the market is so bloody persistent. Is the fact that the market isn't going up still a sign of weakness? If only I knew.

## 1 June 2001

*Market100 at 106.86 and I'm angry and frustrated – why isn't anything happening? – I'm not referring to my weight, which I can change with a bit of determination, but I can't change the markets or can I?*

Phoned Derivatives Brokers, chatted and wanted to soak them in my bearishness. SELL, SELL, SELL – I wanted it to echo all over the city, spread to Wall Street, a bit of panic would be nice. Shake the market, wake the market, that's what I'd like to see.

Phoned some old colleagues at GlobalBank to try to convince them the market was coming down. Sell, you bastards. You're going to look foolish if you don't act now (and all that crap).

'Greg, how are you, you bullish bastard? D'you still believe the market's gonna stay at this level?'

'Thomas, what's all this about? Have you got some info I should know about?'

'Nothing really, just the odd rumours some big players are thinking about selling shares for bonds, selling UK markets and moving into bonds and that sort of crap. I suppose they're worried about the market being a bit overvalued.'

'Interesting, I'll check with some of my clients. I'll get back to you.'

Made a few more calls of the same nature to stir some activity and spread some rumours. A dull market is always crying out for information to trade on. Traders and brokers get bored otherwise. They've spent too much time in the trendy pubs and wine bars lately for them to feel confident. They want to act – trade – make money, feel the power. Let's hope I'm right.

## 8 June 2001

*Market100 at 107.07 – not sleeping too well – no disaster, but I hate to be wrong – am I wrong this time?*

I feel moody and confused. Went to the office. Normal routine stuff. Took Caroline to lunch. Still little change in the market. At lunchtime the market was up 0.19. No need to worry, but it pisses me off that it keeps going the wrong way.

Still nothing from Greg, or anyone else for that matter. No news. No articles about the right time to sell and stick the money in the mattress.

Getting slightly moody because the market keeps rising – now up 0.32.

## 15 June 2001

*Market100 closed at 104.17 – some good signs from my point of view – a few signals from smaller companies that profits are below the hyped expectations – not been sleeping that well this week*

| TRADE CONFIRMATION | |
|---|---|
| **CONTRACT** | JUNE 2001 (EXPIRY) |
| **TYPE** | PUT |
| **TRANSACTION TYPE** | CLOSING SALE |
| **NO. OF CONTRACTS** | 1000 |
| **STRIKE PRICE** | 105 |
| **UNDERLYING INDEX VALUE** | 104.17 |
| **CALL/PUT VALUE** | 0.83 |
| **INTEREST RATE** | |
| **VOLATILITY** | |
| **TOTAL TO PAY/RECEIVE** | £8300 |

Damn, I lost net £19 996 on my second options trade. Options net to date, a negative of £8120.

**Portfolio summary after close of June contracts**

| Current position | Invested | Value |
|---|---|---|
| Shares | 5 225 000 | 5 442 883 |
| Cash | 264 860 | 271 107 |
| Options | 0 | 0 |
| Total value | 5 489 860 | 5 713 990 |
| Total growth | −10 140 | 213 990 (+3.89%) |

Still behind Market100 – lagging by 0.28%. Not disastrous, but I was rather hoping to be able to beat it.

## 29 June 2001

*Market100 at 104.27 at close of business for the day, the month and the second quarter*

Recovered a bit of confidence. Some signal about overvaluation is seeping through, and I think it's a bit more than wishful thinking on my part. I've reassessed the situation and decided to go for the kill a second time. I'm going to build the put position again – would like to have at least 5000 contracts. It would mean spending £137 835, which I was quite willing to do. I considered writing some calls, but decided the overall risk of such a position was too great. I mean, what if the market went up instead of down? I could get seriously hammered.

| TRADE CONFIRMATION | |
|---|---|
| **CONTRACT** | SEPTEMBER 2001 (84 DAYS REMAINING) |
| **TYPE** | PUT |
| **TRANSACTION TYPE** | OPENING PURCHASE |
| **NO. OF CONTRACTS** | 5000 |
| **STRIKE PRICE** | 105 |
| **UNDERLYING INDEX VALUE** | 104.27 |
| **CALL/PUT VALUE** | 2.7567 |
| **INTEREST RATE** | 5% |
| **VOLATILITY** | 15% |
| **TOTAL TO PAY/RECEIVE** | £137 835 PAY |

## 6 July 2001

*Market100 at 105.89 – at least some sunshine – sleeping well – got 25 new clients in the last quarter – smaller accounts though, only matching some minor outflows of funds*

Arrived at the office and Caroline wasn't there. The phone kept ringing, lots of trivial stuff. I put the answerphone on and did my daily routine. Caroline got through on my mobile and said her car had broken down this morning and she couldn't get to the station. She hoped to be in tomorrow. 'You bloody better had,' I said, 'the place is caving in.' A bit exaggerated, but even so.

Another annoying day with the market pretty much unchanged – down 0.04. And still no reaction. What's going on? Or rather, why isn't anything happening? I suddenly realised I don't have the power to talk the market up or down. It's going be a 'wait and see' thing. I was back on earth. Sulking, feeling very suburban, I got on the 5.30 train.

## 13 July 2001

*Market100 at 103.65 – a move, a move would you believe it, might not be anything significant*

A bit of panic in the US markets today, some significant reports were well below expectations and technology shares fell by 5%. The US Market100 did a bit better – only 2.8% down. Should be interesting to see what the newspapers say about this over the weekend – the market could be in for a scare on Monday.

## 16 July 2000

*Market100 opened, down 2.63 and closed at 100.41 – continued down a bit further to close 3.24 units down (3.12% down) – brilliant weekend – best in many months*

Did I love the weekend reading or what! It's all pretty much a game about feelings and interpretation. When the market's bullish it sometimes overlooks bearish news, and vice versa. Now with a bit of bearishness, a few reports below expectations and a bit of sell pressure, all the bearish news is aired. It's obviously and invariably going to be an overreaction, but it won't hide the fact that it seems the market has been a bit highly valued.

I placed a new order for 1000 contracts at 100.50 for the 100 September strike.

| TRADE CONFIRMATION | |
|---|---|
| **CONTRACT** | SEPTEMBER 2001 (67 DAYS REMAINING) |
| **TYPE** | PUT |
| **TRANSACTION TYPE** | OPENING PURCHASE |
| **NO. OF CONTRACTS** | 1000 |
| **STRIKE PRICE** | 100 |
| **UNDERLYING INDEX VALUE** | 100.50 |
| **CALL/PUT VALUE** | 2.7495 |
| **INTEREST RATE** | 5% |
| **VOLATILITY** | 20% |
| **TOTAL TO PAY/RECEIVE** | £27 495 PAY |

## 17 July 2001

*Market100 opened down another 1.47 – all eyes on the US – my pulse is racing*

Down again. Not since the end of last year has Market100 been below 100. Good hint to further selling if a charting signal were to indicate further falls. The train ride in this morning felt really long. I couldn't wait to get to the office and check the markets.

Called Derivatives Brokers just to check activity. Very noisy and lots going on. No time for chatting – 'place your order or get lost' type of market.

Went for an early lunch. Carried on calling people to gauge the magnitude of what was going on.

'Greg, how are things?' I opened.

'Thomas, good to hear from you, not the best of days for a chat as you can imagine. Pleased on your behalf you were right about the market.'

'Thanks, Greg. So what's your view of all this then?'

'It's . . . wait a minute,' there was shouting in the background, 'The bastards have cut rates. Got to go.' Greg hung up.

I turned to my screen and read the news – interest rates were cut in the US by another 0.25%, which wasn't that unexpected. What was unexpected though was a cut of the same magnitude by the Bank of England. The stock markets went into free fall after the news. Normally, it would have been seen as good news by the markets, but this time it was a sign of distress and too little too late.

The Market100 plummeted to 94.03, just to gain a little bit before close; it closed at 94.96.

Caroline and I left early for a glass of bubbly.

## 18 July 2000

*Market100 opened up 1.69 – the US recovered after the initial slaughter – still bearish news coming out – time for bargain hunting*

A little over a week until our summer holidays in France. We've booked a house by the sea in Normandy – really looking forward to some time off with Edward, James and Amanda. I feel relieved I don't work for GlobalBank anymore – markets like this are synonymous with cancelled holidays.

The market recovered during the day. After the initial rally it kept going up, closing at 98.15. It was an overreaction and when this happens all shares take a beating. This opens the way for bargain hunting – looking for shares that have had unjustifiably big falls. People who haven't yet switched, may change from cyclicals to non-cyclicals.

## 20 July 2000

*Market100 at 96.98 and what a week! – not that I've an eating disorder, but food and drink haven't entered my system to anything like normal levels – result a drop of 2lb – reason, job-related stress – it feels very comfortable, I must say*

Volatility, what a beautiful word! It's risen to 35% and I feel great. When the taxi took me to the station this morning, it felt like I was driven in a limo not the Vauxhall it actually was. I decided to close the 5000-contract position at 96.80.

| TRADE CONFIRMATION | |
|---|---|
| **CONTRACT** | SEPTEMBER 2001 (63 DAYS REMAINING) |
| **TYPE** | PUT |
| **TRANSACTION TYPE** | CLOSING SALE |
| **NO. OF CONTRACTS** | 5000 |
| **STRIKE PRICE** | 105 |
| **UNDERLYING INDEX VALUE** | 96.80 |
| **CALL/PUT VALUE** | 10.1814 |
| **INTEREST RATE** | 5% |
| **VOLATILITY** | 35% |
| **TOTAL TO PAY/RECEIVE** | £509 070 RECEIVE |

Very pleased that I hung in there. Staying power! Netted a nice £369 235.

**A new summary before going off on holiday**

| Current position | Invested | Value |
|---|---|---|
| Shares | 5 225 000 | 5 067 205 |
| Cash | 608 600 | 609 431 |
| Options | 27 495 | 68 283 |
| Total value | 5 861 095 | 5 744 919 |
| Total growth | 361 095 (+6.56%) | 244 919 (+4.45%) |

Now, this looks good, Market100 is down 3.02% and the value of Fund1 is up 4.45%. Superb!

I've given Caroline instructions on the day-to-day stuff while I'm away. She did well last time, so I've got no worries. Nothing I can think of has to be done to the position. A two-week holiday, I'm ready for it, baby! France, here we come!

## 10 August 2001

*Market100 at 96.02 – seems to have stabilised at this level – refreshed, nice tan, in good trim, fabulous holiday*

Superb holiday in a little fishing village, completely untouched except for the more recent development of a few villas to let. Our villa was about 100 yards off the beach, with local fishermen selling seafood in their garages along the way. To stay in a hotel has obvious advantages, but so has this. Spent most days on the beach; lucky the weather was spot on for that kind of life. On the way to the beach, we called by the fishermen and placed our orders for the afternoon pick-up. We asked for oysters and champagne. Everything they had was just so good. Can't get it fresher. And the prices, nothing. It's annoying to find everything so much cheaper in France. Beach life, seafood and barbecues – not too testing. Did a few excursions to the D-Day beaches and

Bayeux to have a look at the tapestry. Edward and James thoroughly enjoyed that. Good stuff!

Back to the normality of rainy London. I shouldn't be too rash. The weather's been okay for most of the summer. Just because it was raining today doesn't warrant my wrath. Board meeting next week; Caroline's arranged it and sent out the usual stuff.

## 17 August 2001

*Market100 at 95.71 – the board meeting went well – the market seems to have established itself at this lower level*

The board gave me the go-ahead to start looking for additional staff – good news. Don and I had prepared a short presentation of the autumn marketing campaign, which would incorporate the recruitment of new staff as well as some marketing trips to where the money is. Ben has some good contacts in high places and said he would do what he could. The aim is to have doubled the funds to £10 000 000 by the end of the year. Whatever comes in, thanks to the campaign, will be parked in Fund2, which will shadow Market100 quite simply.

## 24 August 2001

*Market100 at 94.99 – Amanda's signed us up at a gym – still too fat I suppose – that's me, not Amanda*

Some significant bankruptcies last week. Two of the more highly regarded dotcoms threw it in. One of the mobile phone manufacturers announced they were having difficulties meeting the deadline for their latest handset. Oh dear! Otherwise, no major disasters. The cyclical companies are actually holding their game up rather well.

## 21 September 2001

*Market100 closed at 96.85 – time to count the money – my limbs ache – the gym seems to be doing more harm than good – I sleep well after the workout anyway – no immediate sign of weight loss*

| TRADE CONFIRMATION | |
|---|---|
| **CONTRACT** | SEPTEMBER 2001 (EXPIRY) |
| **TYPE** | PUT |
| **TRANSACTION TYPE** | CLOSING SALE |
| **NO. OF CONTRACTS** | 1000 |
| **STRIKE PRICE** | 100 |
| **UNDERLYING INDEX VALUE** | 96.85 |
| **CALL/PUT VALUE** | 3.15 |
| **INTEREST RATE** | |
| **VOLATILITY** | |
| **TOTAL TO PAY/RECEIVE** | £31 500 RECEIVE |

I should have closed a lot earlier with the big position. The deterioration of the time value was quite hefty. Nevertheless, I can add another £4005 to the options account. Thank you, Sir, thank you! So another contract gone.

**Portfolio valuation again**

| Current position | Invested | Value |
|---|---|---|
| Shares | 5 225 000 | 5 060 412 |
| Cash | 640 100 | 645 178 |
| Options | 0 | 0 |
| Total value | 5 865 100 | 5 705 590 |
| Total growth | 365 100 (+6.64%) | 205 590 (+3.74%) |

Still ahead of Market100, which is down by 3.15% on the year to date. Fund1 on the other hand is up 3.74% in value.

I haven't engaged in any new positions yet and according to my prediction of the band 110 to 95, I feel pretty pleased actually. The question is whether I should now start to play the upside or reassess the lower end of the band – could the market fall to 90 or even below? I wouldn't want that to happen.

By doing nothing I would be neutral to Market100, and with no immediate news indicating otherwise, I'll stay that way.

## 28 September 2001

*Market100 at 95.18 end of day – last week in bed, backache, and people say going to the gym is good for you – haven't slept very well, unless newly doped by painkillers*

Some distress signals from the US. The purchasing managers' index is down again, possibly signalling the beginning of a recession. Retail sales are also down and non-farm payroll is down (unemployment up a bit). Interesting to see what the Fed will do, if anything.

Here the manufacturing industry is complaining about the strong pound. The previous cut wasn't enough to push the pound lower. The pound is still something of a safe haven since the euro has failed to rise notably this year. It's gone up a bit against the dollar, but that's mostly due to dollar weakness than pronounced confidence in the euro. Theoretically it should be higher.

The jury is still out whether you should stay in bed or be up walking with a backache. The bed option causes me least pain at the moment, so I'll stay there.

## 5 October 2001

*Market100 at 94.89 – the back is a bit better*

First time back at the office for a week and a half. Starting to get some reaction to the advertisement for a deputy and a new assistant. Had 25 responses so far. Caroline's done a good job sorting them and given each an initial glance. End of October is the deadline, so no need to worry too much at present.

I've done a new assessment of the market for the rest of the year. I think it'll stay within band, with a possible rally towards the end of the year. I'm going to play the bull game. Instead of buying call options, I've decided to write put options at 95 strike. 500 contracts.

Done! 500 at 94.75, which gave me £12 719 in nice little premium money. Volatility has come down to 18%, which isn't too bad. Could have been better, though.

| TRADE CONFIRMATION | |
|---|---|
| CONTRACT | DECEMBER 2001 (67 DAYS REMAINING) |
| TYPE | PUT |
| TRANSACTION TYPE | OPENING SALE |
| NO. OF CONTRACTS | 500 |
| STRIKE PRICE | 95 |
| UNDERLYING INDEX VALUE | 94.89 |
| CALL/PUT VALUE | 2.5438 |
| INTEREST RATE | 5% |
| VOLATILITY | 18% |
| TOTAL TO PAY/RECEIVE | £12 719 RECEIVE |

## 12 October 2001

*Market100 at 94.79 – still no news*

I went back to the gym again this week. The trainer gave me a programme to follow to build up the muscle strength in my back and a diet to reduce the beer belly in front. Combined it should do wonders he said. He may be right, but bloody boring.

I've been bringing a little lunch box to the office for the last two days – bloody tuna, a slice of rye bread (no butter of course) and fruit. Champagne is unluckily not in the diet and neither is Guinness, bitter or a pint of refreshing lager. Water, water and water. Well, tea and coffee without milk and sugar are okay. No restrictions there.

The market seems to have gone back to its steady side movement. Probably won't be much more action until December, when hopefully a bit of bargain hunting will bring the market up a little.

## 17 October 2001

*Market100 slaughter, fell to 89.67 – closed at the lowest point – panic, panic!*

Who said the market had stabilised and was due north? Me, silly me. Like a flash from a clear sky, the US opened a bit lower, then the bottom fell out. I panicked and jumped on the phone to Derivatives Brokers. I had to protect the bloody position. Managed to buy 90-strike puts for 500 contracts valued seriously over their theoretical value, but nothing to do about it.

| TRADE CONFIRMATION | |
|---|---|
| **CONTRACT** | DECEMBER 2001 (55 DAYS REMAINING) |
| **TYPE** | PUT |
| **TRANSACTION TYPE** | OPENING PURCHASE |
| **NO. OF CONTRACTS** | 500 |
| **STRIKE PRICE** | 90 |
| **UNDERLYING INDEX VALUE** | 89.67 |
| **CALL/PUT VALUE** | 6.0258 |
| **INTEREST RATE** | 5% |
| **VOLATILITY** | 35% |
| **TOTAL TO PAY/RECEIVE** | £30 129 PAY |

What I've effectively locked in is a loss of 5% on my written puts. If the market continues down, the position should be neutral. If it goes up, the value of the written options will come back a bit, but the premium paid for the other puts will be lost.

### New valuation

| Current position | Invested | Value |
|---|---|---|
| Shares | 5 225 000 | 4 685 258 |
| Cash | 622 690 | 629 118 |
| Options | 17 410 | 4 723 |
| Total value | 5 865 100 | 5 319 099 |
| Total growth | 365 100 (+6.64%) | −180 901 (−3.29%) |

The market measured by Market100 is down on year to date by 10.33%. Fund1 down by 3.29%.

## 18 October 2001

*Market100 opened slightly up – some late recovery in the US – didn't sleep at all*

It's not over yet! I don't understand what that was all about. Nothing fundamental had changed to warrant the fall. Most people I spoke to were equally baffled.

I was pleased I'd neutralised my position for further falls at a cost. I was short put options at 95 and long put options at 90. The worst-case scenario would be a December close of the contracts around 90. A loss on the short put options without any gains on the long put options at 90. The best would be a close obviously above 95. No loss on the short put, but of course nothing gained from the long put.

## 9 November 2001

*Market100 at 92.32 – all comments are the same – it was an overreaction – lost 5lb, but I'm off the bloody diet now – a working man needs his lunches and so on*

A bit better. Could be worse. What else can I say to cheer me up? Well, the marketing campaign is going well and Ben has arranged for me to go to Riyadh, of all places, to meet some incredibly rich people. Apparently, Ben has sold the idea to them and they want to learn more about derivatives. I've been invited to hold a derivatives workshop for a week. I'm flying out the day after tomorrow – the 11th – and I return the weekend after. No alcohol out there, so I may just as well carry on with the diet. I wonder what they eat and drink in Saudi Arabia.

## 22 November 2001

*Market100 at 94.35, good recovery – I got back safely from Riyadh – in all a very rewarding trip – I kept my weight*

I was told to be patient when passing through immigration upon arrival and not to go to the bathroom. That is apparently one of the signals they look for in the search for smugglers. You'd do pretty much anything to avoid the nasty rubber glove experience. To my surprise, it wasn't all that bad. Only took about 35 minutes to clear immigration and find a taxi to go to the hotel.

The hotel was newly built and very luxurious, close to a fabulous shopping mall and the conference centre where the workshops were to be held.

The shopping mall had everything you could ask for. Harvey Nichols, the obvious souvenir shop and a food court that offered food from all corners of the world. Besides Saudi there was Japanese, Chinese, Italian, Lebanese and, of course, American. American food was represented by Ronald himself, how unusual. Nonetheless, reassuring to know what you get when you order it, simply by pointing at a well-known burger for example.

The hotel had a superb brasserie and a more expensive à la carte restaurant. Without any wine to accompany the food, I settled for the brasserie. Best were the Caesar salad with garlic and chilli prawns and the US cheeseburger. To drink, coke and Saudi champagne had to do. Now, Saudi champagne isn't anything near the real bubbly. It's just a drink of sparkling mineral water, grape juice and fresh fruits. Thirst quenching and not too bad.

One night I was taken out to the desert, which seems to be the place to go in your spare time. I was taken to a hubbly-bubbly, they said. A place with alcoves and mattresses on the floor. Each alcove had a telly, with 80-odd satellite channels to view. The idea was to relax by smoking a water pipe and drinking tea or coffee while zapping around. Being a non-smoker, I took a cautious approach to it, but after a few sucks the apple flavour made it a rather nice experience. It was extremely relaxing apart from all those noisy tellies.

The workshop went very well indeed. The outcome was an initial promise of £3 000 000 to be invested in my funds.

I never had the stomach to go to Chop Chop Square on the Friday morning. Does the French Revolution ring a bell? Nasty business!

Pleased to see the market's recovered a bit.

## 7 December 2001

*Market100 at 93.64 – Christmas time soon again, the year has just flown by – 10lb down, which isn't too bad*

All in all, the campaign has been good once again. New funds exceeding £7 000 000. Just hoping to round off this year without too many injuries from the battlefield.

I'll merge the two funds for next year. No point yet in keeping them apart, since people seem to like the idea of my using derivatives. With the market at current levels it should be a good year.

## 21 December 2001

*Market100 closed at 95.87, not too bad – extremely busy December, have been doing a number of client entertaining activities, which have been well received*

| TRADE CONFIRMATION | |
|---|---|
| **CONTRACT** | DECEMBER 2001 (EXPIRY) |
| **TYPE** | PUT |
| **TRANSACTION TYPE** | CLOSING PURCHASE |
| **NO. OF CONTRACTS** | 500 |
| **STRIKE PRICE** | 95 |
| **UNDERLYING INDEX VALUE** | 95.87 |
| **CALL/PUT VALUE** | 0 |
| **INTEREST RATE** | |
| **VOLATILITY** | |
| **TOTAL TO PAY/RECEIVE** | £0 |

Phew, I got out of the short put position without burning my hands severely. I gained £12 719. But I lost on my panic hedge – all of the £30 129 premium. Overall that's a net loss of £17 410.

| TRADE CONFIRMATION | |
|---|---|
| **CONTRACT** | DECEMBER 2001 (EXPIRY) |
| **TYPE** | PUT |
| **TRANSACTION TYPE** | CLOSING SALE |
| **NO. OF CONTRACTS** | 500 |
| **STRIKE PRICE** | 90 |
| **UNDERLYING INDEX VALUE** | 95.87 |
| **CALL/PUT VALUE** | 0 |
| **INTEREST RATE** | |
| **VOLATILITY** | |
| **TOTAL TO PAY/RECEIVE** | £0 |

I'm pleased with the year and I'm taking a nice quiet holiday en famille over Christmas and New Year.

Happy Christmas and a Happy New Year!

# CHAPTER SIX

## 31 December 2001

*Market100 closed the year at 94.73 – the funds will be merged for the start of next year – yes I gained 2lb over Christmas – yes, it's back to the gym soon – it keeps rolling on*

A successful year in all. Struggled a bit with the recruitment of new staff, but with assistance from a recruitment firm we got it sorted. A nice girl called Wendy Smith will start as new assistant at the end of January and Fred Winther, who has a solid track record from a number of investment banks in both sales and risk management, will be joining us in late February as my deputy.

How did the year end? Well, the following summary should be proof enough that it was a good year.

| **Current position** | **Invested** | **Value** |
|---|---|---|
| Shares | 5 225 000 | 4 949 643 |
| Cash | 647 137 | 647 137 |
| Options | 0 | 0 |
| Total value | 5 872 137 | **5 596 780** |
| Total growth | 372 137 (+6.77%) | **96 780 (+1.76%)** |

An absolutely marvellous first year – outperformed the market by 7.03%. Fund1 gained 1.76% in value, whereas Market100 fell by 5.27%. I feel like Master of the Universe! And moreover, I can add to this another £7 000 000 in new funds. Next year is most certainly going to be just as exciting.

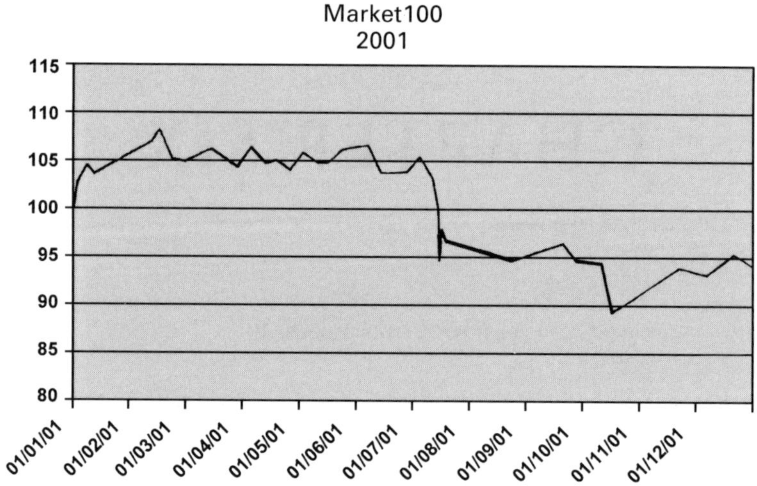


It's worth summarising the year in brief. The market's been mad and bad, but it sobered up a bit as the second half saw an adjustment to more realistic price/earnings ratios. As always the market overreacted and all shares got the slag, even those that actually showed a very good and solid growth in output and profitability.

The first quarter (Q1) started positively from 100 up to 108.62 in mid-February, which was the year high. Market100 then dropped back fairly quickly to a level around 105–106 and ended the quarter at 105.50.

Q2 was boring and a disaster for me. I'd started to develop a bearish view on the market and begun reducing exposure. The quarter ended at 104.27.

Q3 was about existing stuff. It proved the name of the game is staying power. All of a sudden, negativism started to flood the market. The dotcom arena saw a few spectacular bankruptcies. A rapid fall down to 94-ish and a quick recoil back to 98-ish, before closing the quarter at 95.18.

In Q4 what could stop the bear? Nothing – the market fell to its year low of 89.67, which happened to be on 17 October, a date with seriously bad vibes for market professionals. The market sobered up a bit and the index recovered to close at 94.73. Bargain hunting was the name of the game here.

I've learnt a lot during the last year – well last two years actually. I've learnt to believe in myself and to trust my own judgement. I'm not saying I'm always right, but being in fund management and using derivatives forces you to develop a view, a strategy. You must act accordingly and be prepared to re-assess and change that strategy.

On the positive side, I feel I've been more of a husband and father – quite simply a very good balance in life. It's extremely rewarding to have started the business and to have done it successfully. Obviously, there's never time for complacency, and 'continuous improvement' is my new motto.

On the negative side, it has taken time to adjust from a vibrant investment bank environment to a small office of two. There has been uncertainty and anxiety about the success and sustainability of the business, and there still is. However, with a good start and with new staff, much of that will hopefully change.

And life goes on. I've got to develop a view for the year ahead – well I have a view, which I need to firm up. I expect the beginning to be a bumpy ride. There's still a lot of uncertainty out there. The market will slow down and most likely see a modest increase in prices. My range is 90 to 100, possibly 105 towards the end of the year if we're lucky. There's a board meeting coming up in two weeks' time, which will have to be my deadline for this exercise. Quite a bit more to prepare, though. Better get on with it. Not much of the holiday left now, just the party tonight and the usual recovery tomorrow. Got to make the most of it!

# EPILOGUE

The idea with this book was always to explain derivatives to the layman in an easy and understandable way. Derivatives are very complex instruments, and for the purpose of clarity I've glossed over some of their aspects. For example, all calculations have been based on theoretical values, which in real life can diverge from market values or prices, because these are influenced by expectations. Dividends, commissions and other transaction costs have not been included. Frequent trading may generate quite substantial broker bills. Having said that, TR's diary is based on relevant theories for derivatives.

Depending on when you read this book, you may find that the market developments I describe are very different from reality. The idea was never to provide investment advice or to predict the forthcoming market. The idea was to demystify derivatives – to show they can be quite useful when managing portfolios. The story and the market developments are purely fictional, but I think they give a true reflection of how I approach the market, develop the different scenarios and do the calculations.

There are risks associated with everything, even doing nothing. Understanding the risks will significantly increase the readiness and opportunity to address risk, which will increase the chances of better returns. Unfortunately, in many markets, derivatives are treated differently to cash instruments. Derivatives normally have a short life, hence the profits and losses are realised more frequently than for cash instruments. Cash instruments may also have rather lenient accounting rules, leaving unrealised losses and with little or no impact on the bottom line. A continued development to full marking to market and equal treatment of unrealised and realised profits and losses will increase the chances of derivatives being used. As TR's diary explains, derivatives can be used for hedging, arbitraging or even speculating. TR focused on hedging, which makes them more of an insurance instrument.

For those of you who want to learn more about the theory or the practicalities of exchange-traded derivatives, here are some useful books and websites.

*Paul Wilmott on Quantitative Finance* vols 1 and 2, 1998, John Wiley & Sons

*Options, Futures and Exotic Derivatives*, Briys, Bellalah, Mai and de Varrenne, 1998, John Wiley & Sons

*Options as a Strategic Investment*, McMillan, 1986, 2nd edition, NYIF Corp.

www.optionscourse.com – course material for options training courses

www.liffe.com – the home page of the London International Financial Futures and Options Exchange

www.omgroup.com – the home page of the Swedish stock and derivatives exchange

www.eurex.ch – the home page of the German/Swiss exchange